Campaign in the Crimea

Campaign in the Crimea
The Recollections of an
Officer of the 20th Regiment
of Foot

George Shuldham Peard

Campaign in the Crimea: The Recollections of an Officer of the 20th Regiment of Foot
by George Shuldham Peard

First published under the title
Narrative of a Campaign in the Crimea

Leonaur is an imprint
of Oakpast Ltd

Copyright in this form © 2009 Oakpast Ltd

ISBN: 978-1-84677-626-7 (hardcover)
ISBN: 978-1-84677-625-0 (softcover)

http://www.leonaur.com

Publisher's Notes

In the interests of authenticity, the spellings, grammar and place names used have been retained from the original editions.

The opinions of the authors represent a view of events in which he was a participant related from his own perspective, as such the text is relevant as an historical document.

The views expressed in this book are not necessarily those of the publisher.

Contents

Preface	7
To Constantinople	9
Cholera	19
The Crimea	23
The March to Battle	29
The Battle of the Alma	39
The Black River	50
Balaklava	61
Under Fire	69
Before Sebastopol	77
The Line and the Charge	94
Inkermann	103
The Storm	119
I Fall Ill	130
Homeward	140
Conclusions	145

Preface

The following pages are, for the most part, taken from a *Journal* kept, whenever circumstances allowed me to do so, from the time of my departure from England, on the 18th of July, 1854, to my return, on the 12th of January, 1855. This *Journal* was originally intended solely for the perusal of my wife and nearest relations.

If I had seen other books of the same kind published by those who had taken an active part in the campaign, I should speedily have relinquished my task; but, although there are some admirably written letters, especially those of "Our Correspondent" of *The Times* (whose descriptions are as vivid as they are faithful), I have not heard that any "combatant" has hitherto published the result of his own observations; and it has sometimes been thought by me, that, however imperfectly I may have described scenes and incidents worthy of a much abler pen, the following pages might not be wholly uninteresting to the public, because they contain a true and authentic account of what came under my own. observation during the late campaign of this terrible and eventful war.

George Shuldham Peard
Penzance, April, 1865.

Chapter 1

To Constantinople

In the month of July, 1854, the 20th Regiment received orders to embark for service in the East, in the screw steamer *Colombo*. The vessel arrived at Plymouth some days sooner than we expected; and as we were told, on Saturday, the 16th instant, that she would sail on the following Monday, little time remained to prepare the many articles which we required for our expedition. I fear the intervening Sunday was by no means a day of rest to us or to many of the shopkeepers and their workmen, though the work was one of necessity. Some were finishing packsaddles; some pressing tea, groceries, and portable soup into a marvellously small compass; others completing bedsteads of the most convenient form I ever saw, invented by Major C——.

By the bye, it is to be regretted that he did not take out a patent for his clever invention, as everyone who saw them endeavoured to purchase them; and I am convinced that in future campaigns they will be generally used by officers. The barrack-yard presented during the day a most busy appearance,— some anxious to buy, others to sell; some to pay their bills, others to get them paid. There was however a short interval of rest for some of us, who managed to go to church, where we heard a most impressive sermon preached by the excellent chaplain of the garrison.

On Monday morning the regiment mustered 996 strong, and then marched to the victualling yard wharf, where we embarked in four small steamers, which took us to the *Colombo*.

It was a sad sight to see our brave fellows parting, perhaps forever, from those dear to them. There was indeed much cheering as they marched, while the band played its most lively and inspiriting airs; but there were few amongst us who did not feel that they might be leaving their native land for the last time; and, though the soldiers re-echoed the cheers, a general and unmistakable gloom prevailed, which could not have escaped the observation of anyone who has ever witnessed the embarkation of a regiment.

Soon after we had reached the *Colombo*—a fine iron steamer of about 1870 tons, belonging to the Peninsular and Oriental Company,—we were told that she would not sail until the next day. As soon therefore as the men were settled down in their places, and I and two other officers had secured berths together in the same comfortable cabin, many of us obtained leave to go on shore.

After a second sad farewell to my wife and little ones, I embarked again soon after midnight, at which time our ship was being prepared to receive a quantity of ammunition.

I will not weary the reader by recounting the details of a most prosperous voyage, unattended by adventures of any kind; or by attempting to describe the magnificent and apparently impregnable rock of Gibraltar, or the beautiful harbour and town of Valetta. This has often been done before, by abler pens than mine. Suffice it to say that, after a short stay at Malta, we reached Constantinople, on the morning of the 2nd of August,—sixteen days from the day we left Plymouth.

As we approached, the rays of the rising sun gleamed on the domes and minarets of this splendid city, and from the Sea of Marmora a magnificent *coup d'œil* presented itself. The Bosphorus shone like silver in the bright sun, reflecting the high coloured houses and tall dark cypresses. Here and there its surface was broken by the passage of merchantmen and huge transports and steamers.

We were soon anchored in the midst of this beautiful scene, and shortly afterwards I went ashore to ascertain how far the internal condition of Constantinople corresponded with the grandeur of its outward appearance. Grievously disappointed I was. The long, narrow streets were swarming with dogs, and the most dirty of the human race, Turks and Greeks, constantly jostled against me, breathing garlic into my very face. Never do I remember making myself so small as when I walked first through this abominable place. However, our stay here was very short, as we received orders to steam up to Beicos Bay.

The next morning therefore we started, and were up at four a.m. to observe a magnificent sunrise. The surrounding country is very mountainous; and along the sides of the hills, which are covered with tall dark cedars, are terraced gardens, reaching down to the road which skirts the water's edge. The houses were built quite close to the water; indeed so close, that I heard of the corner of one of them being carried away by the bowsprit of a transport, to the excessive surprise of an old Turk, at that moment looking out of his window. The reasons assigned for this droll catastrophe were, that the vessel got rather too close to the shore, was caught by the current, and, swinging round, took the house *en route*.

The sail up to Beicos Bay was very enjoyable; the scenery most splendid. We found other steamers lying there foil of troops, who had received similar orders to ourselves, and we were very soon anchored amongst them. The village from which it derives its name is situated on the Asiatic shore, and is a small, dirty place, the only good thing procurable there being water, of which there is a delicious spring situated close to the water's edge. It was easily conveyed in hose to the shore for the ships' boats, many of which were generally to be seen at the wharf.

The European shore, on which are the villages of Therapia and Buyukdere, is far more picturesque than the opposite coast. The English Ambassador, Lord Stratford de Redcliffe, resides in summer at Therapia. Both are very beautiful places, but I should give the preference to Buyukdere.

The principal houses look out on the water, having nothing to separate them from it but a broad road; and many have a bathing-house built out into this crystal stream.

The favourite amusement here seemed to be lounging about in the cool of the day, in the elegant *caiques*, which tend greatly to animate the scene. These are the only boats used in this country. They are rather crank affairs, though very buoyant, and good weather boats; but you can hardly imagine the fright you put your boatman in if you do not sit down in the bottom, on his cushions, perfectly quiet. This is a rather difficult undertaking, while numerous companions are tormenting you. If you are fortunate in your choice of a *caique*, it is a very luxurious way of travelling; but previous to embarkation it is well to ascertain whether the boatmen have been indulging in garlic, of which they are very fond, and eat great quantities.

I was much amused one day at the mode an old Greek in a *caique* adopted to keep his clothes dry in a shower of rain. He was rowing leisurely down in the middle of the Bosphorus, when rain came on. Hereupon the fellow immediately pulled off all his clothes, and shoving them into the locker in the stern of the boat, rowed quietly on: it was lucky that he did so, for it rained in torrents.

We received orders at Beicos to remain there, as the cholera was so bad at Varna, and many men, both of the fleet and army, were falling victims to it. The *Agamemnon* and ships of war belonging to the Allies, were lying near Buyukdere.

Around Beicos the country is very uncultivated, but the soil good. The Sultan's Valley is exceedingly picturesque, and studded with the finest plane-trees I have ever seen, far surpassing those in America. Under these could be seen at intervals a small camp of Turkish soldiers, with their neatly pitched tents of purest white, while here and there a light green one relieved the eye. *Arabas* also, or Turkish wagons, were seen, with their cream-coloured oxen, conveying women and children for their daily drive. They are painted red or some other glaring colour, with gilt wreaths and leaves all over them, and have awnings and fringed curtains to protect the travellers from the sun. It certainly must be good exercise to ride in them, for they are the roughest description of conveyance.

We walked through the cemetery, a large place, full of turbaned headstones, mementos of bearded Turks; those of the women are quite plain. Tall cedars, with their dark foliage, threw a gloom over the place, and the chirping of the cricket and grasshopper grated on our ears.

Swift little Turkish steamers run to and fro from Buyukdere to Constantinople, with their odd mixtures of pretty Greeks' faces, Turkish *yashmaks*, and their fezzed brethren, intermingled with a few English and French officers on-leave. The *yashmaks* of the women are generally small and thin. Probably the period is not distant when it may become merely a fashionable part of woman's dress; an air-woven web, worn only to set off to advantage that which it is now supposed to conceal.

I started early one morning, with some of my brother officers, for Stamboul, in one of these steamers; and they performed the passage of ten miles, including stoppages, in little more than an hour.

On landing, we hired some saddle-horses and rode off to see the bazaars. These are composed of corridors running one into another, and are full of Turks, Greeks, Armenians, and Egyptians. They are very cool, and on this account much resorted to, for they are among the few places the sun cannot reach: a rare occurrence to find a place of this sort in Constantinople. We met a great many Englishmen lounging about, in a costume neither European nor Oriental, but an absurd mixture of both; many had a straw hat and turban.

In passing through the bazaars, we were much pestered by the importunity of the beggars, but found the small boys the most troublesome. One old beggar hunted us wherever we went, pulling and kissing our coat-tails. At first we thought he wanted to pick our pockets, but found *bakshish* (money) was what he wanted.

The shops resemble our stalls at fairs. In front is a platform, on which the Turks sit, who salute you as you pass with a "*Bono Johnny*," and offer their goods to you at twice their value, with the most unblushing impudence. Some few are seen hard at work, which, generally speaking, is not the case, for they are most lazy fellows, and are much oftener to be found reclining in an easy attitude, smoking their pipes. I made it a rule never to offer more than one-half or two-thirds of what they asked for anything, and generally my offer was accepted. The Slipper Bazaar is very well arranged; here they sell nothing else, and the variety of colour and uniformity of arrangement is particularly pleasing. I thought this and the embroidery shops the most attractive part of the bazaar.

I went to see the jewellery, but was afraid to invest my money there, although many very handsome things were exhibited, and there was much temptation to do so. I made most of my purchases at an Armenian's called "Zenope," and I think most Englishmen do the same. His articles are very good, and, though costly, I do not think he ever took a lower sum than he asked. He gave us some delicious lemon ices, which were most refreshing. We afterwards rode some little distance to the Harness Bazaar, in order to purchase saddle-bags, etc., for the campaign; but we found it a miserable open street, and were glad to get out of it as soon as our purchases were made.

The usual plan of thrashing these fellows on their shoulders and legs with a stick is good when they are very exorbitant in their prices. I have frequently seen this mode of treatment produce the desired effect of bringing them to something like fair dealing.

On our return we passed a large barrack, the walls of which were fall of pigeon-holes, where these birds remain perfectly undisturbed, as they are held in great veneration by the Turks. I believe there is an entire mosque, of which they are the undisputed tenants; and I was told that they are fed by the bounty of an old man, who left a legacy for that purpose.

The porters of Constantinople are extraordinary-looking fellows, and carry the most enormous weights on their backs. They wear very tightly-laced gaiters, probably to prevent their breaking down; and they walk along with their hands on their knees, a plan which enables them to carry a much heavier load.

A dozen of these fellows, with their long, springy poles, are capable of carrying a ton weight. When one man is employed, he generally has a friend to clear the road, when not taking his turn at the burden.

We visited the mosque of Santa Sophia, which, after we had taken off our shoes, we were allowed to enter. It is certainly very magnificent; the dome adorned with noble pillars of the rarest marble; but I must confess that I was disappointed with it, after all I had heard of its splendour. Large green shields of wood, with gilt letters and characters, were hung round the edifice; and here and there, in a kind of railed altar, might be seen a priest throwing himself into all sorts of attitudes . and uttering a mournful cry, whilst a small urchin assisted in a most lugubrious yell, which I presume he imagined was singing.

We were very glad to leave Constantinople that afternoon, being heartily tired of its dirty streets, swarming with dogs and filthy inhabitants, and smelling of every kind of putrefaction. Being late for our dinner on board ship, we decided on dining at the *table d'hôte* at Buyukdere, and remaining to hear the band of the Rifle Brigade perform in the evening. This was a great treat, for a finer military band I never heard. During our stay at Beicos they delighted us very often, and the music sounded sweet across the water.

Every morning before breakfast was employed in bathing; K—— almost lived in the water, being an excellent swimmer, but it was not a very pleasant place for a bad one, as there was no sand, and the stones were very sharp.

The weather now became most oppressively hot, and we were compelled to protect our heads from the scorching sun by winding a long white turban round our straw hats and wide-awakes. Above all things, we found our white cotton umbrellas, which we bought at Malta, most useful. Two of our men died on board ship of cholera; the other regiments around us suffered a good deal more. As we were likely to remain here some time, application was made to the Sultan to allow our men to be encamped on the Asiatic shore. This was very soon granted, and we were landed, and made our camp on a beautiful hill, overlooking the Black Sea and the Bay in which our ship was lying.

Happily the cholera did not visit us here, although the Rifle Brigade and the 63rd Regiment (which were encamped some little distance from us) were very unfortunate, particularly the former, whose funeral parties were constantly seen marching down the hill to the place of interment. Our men enjoyed their move very much, and received their rations from the ship, but the officers went on board for their meals, boats being constantly employed in taking them to and from the steamer. The arrangements made by the purser and officers of the *Colombo* were admirable, and to them we are indebted for the comforts and attention we received during the two months we lived on board her. The soldiers were all sent down to the Bosphorus to bathe every morning, after parade, which was a very salutary arrangement.

I rode one day to Kulalee with an officer of the 63rd Regiment, where the Scots Greys and the Fourth Division of Artillery were quartered, and on our way we passed through the Valley of the Sweet Waters of Asia. Here were assembled numbers of men, women, and children, who, we were informed, resorted thither once a week. Some of them were to be seen sitting beneath the plane-trees in picturesque groups, whilst others drove slowly about in their phaetons and pair, or in *arabas* drawn by cream-coloured oxen. Groups were also assembled in a circle around two or three musicians, who were singing and playing on some extraordinary instruments: a more discordant noise I never before heard. On approaching this assembly we were warned to retire quietly, by an old Turk, who, holding up his hands, shook his head at us, and informed us that we were not to enter the circle. Shortly after we left this place we met the *cortége* of the Sultan, which consisted of eight or ten carriages.

I was very glad of this fine opportunity of forming an idea of Eastern beauty; and certainly was very much surprised at it, as the women I had hitherto seen were truly anything but good-looking. The whole train of carriages stopped as we were passing them, and a pretty, thinly-veiled lady commenced chattering and laughing with her companions. From her gesticulations she appeared much to admire my companion's little horse, which I was riding. The black attendants, who rode between each carriage, were highly amused, grinning and showing their white teeth and eyeballs, at the same time spurring and making the most of their little horses: they are conceited, fat, lubberly fellows.

The ladies were very pale, with large black eyebrows, and small white hands; their *yashmaks* are of the thinnest material and quite transparent, and are generally removed from their faces whenever an opportunity offers. On this occasion we were particularly fortunate in getting a long look at many a pretty face. Passing a large house on the road home, D—— spied a rose, as he thought, stuck in the blind of a window. This he immediately seized, amidst the gesticulations of some fair inmates, but lo! it was a piece of pink calico! An old Turk in a bow-window opposite was dreadfully irate at the proceeding, and a Greek passing by informed us by signs that it was "*no bono*," and highly improper.

One day I with three other officers rode to the forest of Belgrade, about ten miles from Buyukdere. It was here that Lady Mary Wortley Montagne resided for some time. On the road we passed under a very ancient aqueduct, which conducts water into Constantinople, but there was no date to enable us to trace its antiquity. Some little way further, in the centre of a wood, we came to a large reservoir, from which the water was carried into the capital of the Eastern world.

There was a summer residence here, which was shut up at the time we saw it: it appeared a most suitable locality for a picnic. We dismounted at a small cottage close by, a kind of shop, and ordering some coffee, which we found most horrible stuff, but producing the cold meat and biscuit from our haversacks, we had a most sumptuous repast under the trees. The shopkeeper, an old Turk, amused himself by winding a long sash round his waist, into which he stuck a pistol of a very large size. Not knowing our friend very well, we drew our revolvers and commenced cocking them, to show him that we were also prepared for the worst; whereupon he came up and admired them very much. Continuing our ride still further, but finding nothing particularly worth seeing, we picked some grapes in a vineyard, and rode back to the ship, rather disappointed, as our expectations had been much raised with regard to the beauties of the Forest of Belgrade.

We remained in Beicos Bay until the 29th of August, when we received orders to embark the men and horses; and sailing down to Kululee Barracks, took the *Shooting Star* in tow, having on board some artillery and a number of horses.

CHAPTER 2

Cholera

We were all excitement at the move which was now taking place; and the idea of our final destination being revealed to us, inspired us with fresh vigour. It was evident that something was very speedily about to be done, as the transports and steamers were all on the move, and were under orders for Varna. Sebastopol was said by many to be our destination; Kaffa was also spoken of; and some even said that Anapa was to be attacked; while the opinion of others was, that no place at all was to be taken, but that the troops were to be all sent down to winter-quarters at Scutari.

The men had been practised in the embarkation and disembarkation of guns, etc., on the south side of Varna Bay, at which Lord Raglan, Sir Edmund Lyons, and Sir George Brown, were present, and their operations were most successful.

The accounts of the cholera at this time were truly heart-rending. The army suffered dreadfully; but those who have only witnessed the effects of this fatal pestilence on land, can scarcely imagine the horrors of it on board ship. Let the reader picture a thousand men cooped up in a floating cage, the severity of the weather obliging them to close the ports and hatches, thereby, with the exception of what may be obtained by windsails, excluding all pure air from the decks below, and retaining that which was abominably tainted! More than fifty robust men, in the prime of life, were soon removed from their companions, and snatched away by this terrible calamity! No one can describe the horrors of these scenes. It made the stoutest heart indeed quail, to see noble fellows seized by this pestilence, and almost always falling victims, when once they became encircled in its deadly grasp.

Of our ships, the *Britannia* suffered most, losing about one hundred men. This was to be attributed to the admiral's ship being overcrowded with supernumeraries. The *Furious* lost about twenty; the *Trafalgar* thirty-five; the *Albion* fifty; the *Montebello* and another French ship suffered still more, losing about two hundred men each. The work of death had commenced, in many instances before a complaint was made, or any medicine administered.

The British army was scattered all over the country, from Monastir to Varna, a distance of twenty-five or twenty-six miles. The Light Division was encamped at Monastir; but the regiments of which it was composed were scattered widely from each other, and stretched almost from Pravadi to the plains of Monastir. The cavalry brigade, under Lord Cardigan, was at Kosladscki; and the Second Division, which was commanded by Sir De Lacy Evans and which was more healthy than any other, was encamped between Aladyn and Devna: the latter place is called by the Turks the "Valley of Death."

So completely was the brigade of Guards, consisting of about 3000 men, exhausted by sickness and the depressing climate, that they took two days to march ten miles from Devna to Varna, without their packs, which were carried for them. The Highland Brigade was in much better condition; but the Duke of Cambridge had lost one hundred and sixty men, one hundred of whom belonged to the Guards; and before their march to Varna, they had six hundred men sick. The Light Division lost about one hundred and thirty men; Second Division one hundred; Third Division upwards of a hundred; and the cavalry were much reduced. After the great fire at Varna, on the 10th of October, however, the worst seemed to have passed; but no one can look back on those times without the greatest horror at the scenes he witnessed, and without gratitude for having escaped the deadly pestilence.

The fire at Varna caused great destruction of streets and buildings, but more especially of Government stores. In addition to the biscuit and all kinds of provisions which were destroyed, about 19,000 pairs of boots for the soldiers were consumed. There was a great deal of plundering by our own men, but the Zouaves particularly distinguished themselves, being most skilful in that art.

The whole beach was afterwards covered with a great quantity of broken timbers, the remains of the houses which had given shelter to four or five thousand people. Shortly afterwards, a Greek was captured while endeavouring to raise another fire; and it was thought necessary to place a military cordon around the powder-magazines. There is little doubt but the Emperor of Russia had spies at Varna, and that if anything unusual occurred, he received due and timely intimation of it. These spies were in all probability Greeks, who are capable of any villainy.

The preparations for the expedition proceeded with extraordinary activity towards the end of October, both at Constantinople and Varna; but the real object of the expedition still remained a very great mystery. There was, however, little doubt but that a landing in the Crimea was contemplated; but it was generally considered to be rather too late in the season for an undertaking of such magnitude. The supposed expedition to Sebastopol had gained precedence of every other topic of conversation; but certainly the generals succeeded in keeping it a profound secret, which, after all, was most necessary.

The armament of which the expedition was composed was 26,000 French, and nearly as many English. To these may be added about 15,000 Turks or Tunisians. The men were in the highest possible spirits on their march into Varna, to embark on board ship. Their packs were carried on mules and horses, and they sang songs the greatest part of the way, except through Devna, or the "Valley of Death" through which they marched in mournful silence; for it was here that they suffered so much, and left so many of their comrades. Some of the bodies were still lying uncovered, having been dug up by the Bulgarians for the sake of the blankets in which they had been buried. The corps of Bashi Bazouks, which was raised by Colonel Beatson, turned out a failure; for it was found impossible to drill these disorderly rascals into soldiers. They are ferocious-looking fellows, but very cowardly, and ran away whenever an opportunity offered itself.

On the 29th the brigade of Guards and the Highlanders embarked on board the *Simoom, Kangaroo* and other steamers, and went off to those ships, a thousand at a time, in small vessels of light draught of water, which the Government had purchased of Austrian Lloyd's, and which had been built for the navigation of the Danube. The 28th and 44th Regiments, and several others, embarked also on that day, and transports left for Baltschik.

It was stated that, a few days before, a Council of War had been summoned by Marshal St. Arnaud, for the purpose of deciding whether it was prudent to embark the army in its present unhealthy condition. Nothing short of the physical impossibility of carrying out the expedition could justify the postponement or abandonment of a duty which had been ordered to be performed, and which was expected of us by our country. It seems strange, however, that Varna should have been chosen, or rather recommended to us as an encampment for our troops, for the country around is particularly unhealthy, owing to the low marshy ground which surrounds it, from which arise dense fogs and exhalations, engendering malaria, ague, and low fever. Was there no other more suitable or less noxious place in Turkey where the army could have remained, until required for the great expedition which was in contemplation? Whoever recommended it, could not have been a friend either to us or our country, for he must have well known the fatal adversaries with which our army would have to contend.

Chapter 3

The Crimea

On the 1st of September, at twelve a.m., we sailed from Beicos Bay for Varna, with the transport *Shooting Star* in tow, which had on board some of the artillery of the Fourth Division. She was a very fine ship, and did not seem to impede us very much in our course. In the afternoon a poor fellow fell overboard; and although the ship was stopped, and both ships' boats lowered in an incredibly short space of time, we never saw him after he had passed our tow-lines; and I fear that the other ship must have struck him, as we were going very fast through the water.

We arrived at Varna the following morning, at eight o'clock, and saw many line-of-battle ships, and frigates of the combined fleets, sailing out of the bay, which was full of the finest ships England ever sent out, assembled here for the one great purpose, still kept a profound secret, though we were beginning to feel confident that Sebastopol was our destination. There is some reason to believe that the Russians rather expected us at Odessa, for Krusenstern ordered the inhabitants to reduce the city to ashes, if the Allies should attempt to take it, and then to retire to Peraspol, and his proclamation concludes with these words,

"Woe to those who remain behind, or attempt to extinguish the fire!"

When we arrived at Varna our anxiety was much relieved, after the accounts we had lately received about the cholera at that place, on being assured that it was abating both in the army and fleet. After breakfast, the steamer *Harbinger* arrived with our General, Sir George Cathcart, on board, and our men gave him a hearty cheer as he passed. Shortly afterwards, the *Golden Fleece* arrived from England, with the 21st Fusiliers on board. Some of my brother officers went ashore, but soon returned, disgusted with the place, which they said was the most wretched hole they had ever seen.

As the troops were embarking, there was great bustle and confusion. Horses were running loose by dozens on the shore, their owners being unable to take them. One of my friends told me that he had been offered a very good horse for an ounce of tobacco! Many dead bodies, victims to the cholera (which had been raging here fearfully), were seen floating about, having burst out of the hammocks and blankets in which they had been buried.

When the day came for our departure, we were in high spirits, and as the morning of the 5th of November dawned upon us we were under steam, and busily employed in taking once more in tow our old friend the *Shooting Star,* which we had cast off previous to anchoring. The combined fleet and transports soon steered towards Bait-Schick, where we were to assemble in order of battle. It was about eight or ten miles distant, so that it did not take us long to run up. A great many sail of the line and transports had already taken up their position, and anchored.

The village of Baltschick is, like the generality of Turkish towns, a miserable little place. During our stay here, we amused ourselves in paying visits to our numerous acquaintances in the other ships around us. We made up crews, and rowed about whenever the boats could be spared. Here we saw a great number of boats full of dead bodies, which were being conveyed on shore for interment. Everyone seemed to be glad that the great crisis was at hand; and we all trusted that Sebastopol would soon fall, and that we should return to Old England, and sitting over our winter fires, smoke the pipe of peace! All were was anxious to be off; and at last the order for the sailing of the great combined movement arrived, and the day named was the 8th of September.

Our rendezvous was to be "Serpents Island," and at twelve a.m. on that day, we were all in our places in the following order:—

Light Division: chequered or rendezvous flag at the fore; Commander W. Boys; steamers, *The Emperor, Victoria,* and *Andes*; transports, No. 60, 39, 98, 89, 42, 43, 44, 21, 78, and 50.

First Division: blue triangular flag at the fore; Commander Rawstorne, R.N.; steamers, *Tonning, Kangaroo,* and *Emu;* transports, No. 3, 4, 7, 10, 14, 19, 23, and 47.

Second Division: white triangular flag at the fore, Commander E. W. Franklin, R.N.; steamers, *City of London, Melbourne,* and *Hydaspes*; transports, No. 71, 90, 91, 31, 32, 88, 51, and 82.

Third Division: red triangular flag at the fore; Commander Hoseason, R.N; steamers, *Tynemouth, Cambria,* and *Medway*; transports, No. 46, 53, 55, 93, 96, 97, 28, and 6.

Fourth Division: red with white fly, triangular flag at the fore; commanding agent, Lieutenant Wylde; steamers, *Orinoco, Colombo, Avon,* and *Golden Fleece*; transports, No. 37, 58, 48, 56,57, 83,81,20, and 9.

Fifth Division: blue with red fly, triangular flag at the fore; commanding agent, Lieutenant Dicken; steamers, *Simla, Himalaya, Trent,* and *Jason*; transports, No. 1, 34, 40, 61, 85, 2, 36, and 59.

A fair wind and smooth sea enabled the vessels to take their places without confusion or any serious accident, but we were not allowed to steam beyond six knots an hour. On the following day we were off the mouths of the Danube. This day was spent in allowing the ships which had lost ground during the night, to regain their former positions, signal being made to "dress ahead;" and at five p.m. we anchored at our rendezvous, the "Island of Serpents." Here the fleet rallied, and the *Fury* returned from Sebastopol, having been there on a reconnaissance. While on this exciting expedition, she was nearly disabled, receiving a shot in her engine-room. A friend of mine, who was on board, had a cup of coffee knocked out of his hand by the force of the concussion. Sir Edmund Lyons, and Sir George Brown went down in the *Agamemnon,* on a similar voyage of discovery, and report goes, that whilst there the two last-named personages were seen in a state of great anxiety, one at one masthead and another at the other.

On the 10th we made an unsuccessful trip to the *Emperor* for letters, and finished the day by a visit to the *Himalaya,* which we enjoyed very much. She is a noble ship, and well fitted for the conveyance of horses. She had the 8th Hussars and part of the 17th Lancers on board, together with Lord Cardigan and his staff. The *Simla* was there with the 4th Dragoons; the *Jason,* with the 13th Light Dragoons; and the *Trent,* with the 11th Hussars.

A good many men of our regiment died here of cholera, though until this period they had been comparatively free from it. To be confined in a ship with cholera, with deaths frequently occurring, and not knowing whose turn it might be next to be struck by this pestilential disease, is anything but an enviable position. We lost several men during the voyage from Baltschick to Eupatoria.

In the evening of the 11th we started in our former order. It was a beautiful night, and the water as clear as crystal. At six a.m. on the 12th the shores of the Crimea, the scene of our future conquests and sufferings, appeared in sight, and that evening we anchored about five miles from land. The combined fleet passed by, and took up its position around us. At night the divisions were distinguished by the numbers of lights the ships carried at the mastheads; and their reflection in the water made us imagine ourselves in St. James's Park. We received orders to sail early on the next morning, and at one p.m. were close off Eupatoria.

An hour and a half afterwards our regiment received orders from Lord Raglan to land; but at 4.30 it was counter-ordered, to our great delight, as we feared we should miss that grand sight, the fall of Sebastopol, which everyone then thought was so near. The *Caradoc* proceeded towards land with a flag of truce at the fore, and sent a boat ashore; but she returned with Lord Raglan in an hour, giving us another order to land in the morning. At midnight we received a counter-order from Sir Edmund Lyons to sail at two the following morning, and to steer E.S.E. eight miles to rendezvous. During the day the *Britannia* sailed past us, and our band struck up "Rule Britannia." She acknowledged the compliment by playing "British Grenadiers," and many a hearty cheer passed between both vessels.

Eupatoria is a thriving commercial town, with a population of 10,000 to 11,000 inhabitants, principally Crim Tartars, with a sprinkling of Greeks, Armenians, and Karaite Jews. With the exception of some low hills encircling the town, the surrounding country is peculiarly level and destitute of trees, being principally pasturage for vast herds of sheep and oxen, and by no means extensively cultivated by the Tartars. Towards the south, there are about fifty windmills. The houses have a picturesque appearance from the sea, with their red-tiled roofs, and one or two pointed minarets rising behind them. There is but little water in the harbour, which, unlike Sebastopol, is never frozen over, and affords hardly any shelter for ships. Eupatoria is called Genlev by the Tartars, and its Russian name is Korsloff.

As we approached, crowds of people could be discerned gathered before an important-looking building, with white columns and a dome, evidently watching our movements with interest. But it was soon apparent that no hostile demonstrations were intended, and the good people of Eupatoria seemed marvellously little discomposed by the sudden appearance of such a mighty armament in their usually peaceful waters. As soon as it became dark, we saw telegraphs on the coast at work. These were composed of several lights, the number of which was changed according to the message.

The trade from this port is principally black Astrachan wool, which is sent off in great quantities to all parts of the world. The sheep are of a peculiarly small breed: I have frequently seen them taken up and carried in one hand.

At two a.m. on the morning of the 14th we all moved off in order, under cover of the darkness; and the combined fleets, with the steamers and transports, soon anchored in Kalamita Bay, in the most perfect manner, and without the slightest confusion; with this exception, that through some mistake the French steamers took up the buoys we had laid down for our ships, consequently we were left without any, and the French landed first. The French tricolour was planted on the shore at nine o'clock in the morning. The only persons who appeared to wish to oppose our landing were half-a-dozen Cossacks, who stationed themselves on the top of a high bank, and remained there with their horses as long as it was prudent, looking at us with great composure through their glasses. We returned the compliment, and they afforded us at any rate a little amusement.

We were however not long behind the French in landing, and the 23rd Royal Welsh Fusiliers had the honour of reaching land first, being in the Light Division. Shortly afterwards the Rifles were seen advancing and throwing out skirmishers along the shore. The boats came to our ship in the middle of the day, and putting our three days' provisions, biscuit and pork, into our haversacks, together with a great-coat and blanket strapped to our backs, we landed without an accident of any kind.

CHAPTER 4

The March to Battle

Certainly nothing could be more promising than the weather on the day of our landing. It was indeed a grand sight to witness the crowds of boats, each carrying the flag of its division, discharging their living freight upon the beach, each one flushed with the hopes of speedy success.

Soon after the 23rd had landed, Sir George Brown and one or two other officers, who were tempted to reconnoitre a little too far, were very nearly taken prisoners by some Cossacks, and were obliged to beat a speedy retreat. All the divisions moved up to high ground except the Fourth, the one to which I belonged. We were left on the narrow strip of beach which separates the Salt Lake from the sea, where we had landed. It was a very low, unhealthy spot, and our men suffered much from cholera, which generally carried them off after three or four hours' illness. We now took up our position for the night, just before dusk, and piled our arms. At dusk our men lay down under them, for the first night's campaign in the Crimea. Before our first hour's sleep however had passed over, we were aroused by a drenching rain, and before long were wet to the skin; so there was nothing left for us but to congregate around the huge bonfires the men had made out of the broken barrels and planks they had picked up upon the beach.

Of all the miserable nights I ever spent in my life, this was the most wretched: its discomforts it would be impossible to describe. It gave us a little foretaste of the comforts we were likely to enjoy in the Crimean campaign. Shelter there was none, for officers or men; I believe Sir George Brown was fortunate enough to sleep under a bullock-wagon. A misty exhalation arose from the lake, which caused much sickness among our men. The following day we were almost baked by a broiling sun, which struck down on our heads with double strength.

At an early hour the cavalry and artillery commenced landing, and the disembarkation of troops continued with great activity all day. Staff officers, with cocked hats, were to be seen galloping about in all directions. There was a heavy surf running, which made it very difficult to land horses. Several boats were upset and dashed to pieces by the sea on the beach, and some horses were drowned, either by jumping out of the boats or by their being upset. It was a very exciting sight. A boat-load of mules caused much amusement. As the sailors drove them out of the boat with the oars, they jumped and floundered on the soft sand one over the other, to the great amusement of the sailors, who were in great force on this occasion. Each sailor seemed to do the work of two men, and the greatest credit is due to them and their officers, for their persevering and indefatigable labours at the landing. Sir Edmund Lyons was to be seen running up and down the beach, giving his orders to the boats. He had the management of all, and most efficiently did he see that his commands were carried out.

The dew at night was very heavy, as I experienced, being on picket duty, some distance in rear of our division. The following day was far better adapted for landing the horses and artillery, as the sea had greatly subsided, and there was hardly any surf running on the beach. This enabled the tars to do double the work of the previous day.

The spring from which our men procured water was about a mile from the camp, in the direction of Eupatoria, and the road between it and our halting-place was always thronged with soldiers. They seldom walked both ways, as they managed to find kind friends there, who, strange to say, gave them ponies on which to return. These were offered for sale as soon as they had performed their duties, and were to be purchased for a few shillings.

As I was marching one day, with my three days' provisions, blanket, and great-coat, on my back, I found that it would be impossible for me to become my own pack-horse during a long march. Having expressed a wish for a pony in the hearing of some of the men, a pair were brought for me, the very next morning, to choose from, one of which K—— and I purchased for a few shillings; and after his tail was banged and mane hogged, no person would have recognized him. He had eight very large letters, L.K.XX. and G.P.XX., cut on his back, to prevent his being stolen. This pony turned out a most serviceable animal, and accompanied us through the whole campaign. Shortly after our purchase, a strict order was issued by Lord Raglan, forbidding any recurrence of such transactions.

As soon as we had established our pony, the next thing was to send to the ship for the saddle-bags. We each decided on taking a clean pair of socks and a flannel shirt, together with boots, etc., and making ourselves as comfortable as circumstances would admit. We also took with us a coffee-grinder, as the coffee was issued unground, in the bean. I went to the ship for the pack-saddle and saddle-bags. The latter articles are generally made of leather or horsehair, and are always used by the Turks slung over the cantle of their saddles, resembling two carpet-bags, tied together at the handles. They are most useful articles, and I would recommend any one travelling in the East always to purchase "the real natives" at Constantinople, at the Saddle Bazaar. From the comfort our pony afforded to two or three of us, by carrying our coats, etc., I often thought it was to be regretted that the officers of each regiment were not allowed to take three or four of these ponies from Varna, where perhaps 2000 had been left to starve upon the beach. Subsequently they would have proved most useful (as our pony did) in assisting to transport biscuit and pork from Balaklava to the camp before Sebastopol, when the Commissariat had no other means of obtaining provisions.

Our brigadier-general, Goldie, had not arrived in time to

take command on landing, and therefore Colonel Horn, 20th Regiment, was appointed to the temporary command. He appointed Major Sharpe, 20th Regiment, his brigade major, and Captain Radcliffe, 20th Regiment, his *aide-de-camp*. Lieutenant-Colonel Crofton then took command of the regiment.

The 17th was Sunday, so we had church-service and parade on the beach, and an excellent sermon from one of our chaplains: comforts with which we were seldom blessed afterwards. After church K—— and I bathed in the sea, which we found most refreshing, as the heat was intense. That day we asked another officer to dine with us, and we sat, or rather lay down, in our tent, which had just been pitched close to the beach, to a capital dish of soup, and a shoulder of mutton, which my worthy brother officer and messmate had purloined from the kitchen on board ship. This was a thoroughly good meal, and we enjoyed it much after living for two days on pork and biscuit. K—— proved himself a capital cook; to him indeed I was indebted for many a good repast.

On the 18th we lost three men by cholera, each after a very short illness. Our regiment was sent on picket, about half a mile to the rear, but we were drawn in nearer at night. Now and then we saw long droves of bullocks and dromedary wagons pass through the camp, escorted by *spahis*, laden with hay and corn, having, together with numbers of oxen, sheep, and horses been captured and driven in. These *spahis* are strange-looking fellows. They accompany the French army, and are principally used by them for escort and foraging duties. They go by the name of "Old Women" in our army; and certainly they strongly resemble them, from the hoods affixed to their cloaks being generally drawn over their heads. They ride very small horses, which are excessively active, and answer most admirably their sharp bits. When they passed our camp, they were generally received with a shout of laughter.

That night we lay down at our arms, and some of us made a bed of straw, and patched up a capital cover with a few old hoops and waterproof sheets; but unfortunately we had an unpleasant neighbour, in the shape of a dead horse, which had been washed on shore and lodged on the beach close to our halting-place. Not being able to remove him, he became very obnoxious, and the stench in the morning was almost intolerable. At six a.m. on the following day we received orders to march into camp, and to remain there until we saw the flag dropped at head-quarters on the hill, when the First Brigade of the Fourth Division was to advance.

Orders had been issued on the previous night, that the troops should strike tents at daybreak, and that they should be sent on board ship, as it was determined that the army should advance. It was ascertained that the Russian cavalry and Cossacks had been laying waste the country, sweeping off the supplies, and burning all the houses that lay in our march. The boats lined the beach, for the reception of the tents, etc., and the Second Brigade of the Fourth Division, under Brigadier-General Torrens, was ordered to remain behind until the beach was cleared of them.

We now marched into camp, and when we arrived we found all hurry, bustle, and confusion. Uncooked rations were served out to the men, which some were unwilling to carry, while others, in the hurry to stand to their arms, were unable to obtain their portion. This was a great pity; for I believe half the men of our regiment started without water in their kegs, to which in a great measure must be attributed the number who fell out during the march. The well was too far from the camp to allow them to fetch it that morning before they commenced their march; and considering the total absence of water in our line of march it should have been provided, and boats sent ashore with it from the ships, a very few of which would have been sufficient for their wants.

Our men thus started uncomfortably, and without their breakfasts, for which no time was allowed them. I fortunately had a small piece of cold boiled pork and biscuit in my haversack. This, and a pull at my water barrel, composed my *déjeûner*. On arriving at head-quarters we found our general, Sir George Cathcart, waiting for us, and were all much inspirited by his active and soldierlike appearance. As soon as the wagon-train and commissariat carts arrived, and had passed on to some little distance, we marched. It was a very hot, sultry morning, and the sun struck down op our poor heads with unusual violence. Our pace in marching was obliged to be regulated with great judgement, as we were on a vast plain, without even a drop of water, or shade of any kind. A more monotonous country I never beheld, and we had fifteen miles of it. The order of march was as follows:—

                      Cavalry,—8th, 11th, 17th.
Light Division   Artillery   Second Division.
First Division   Artillery   Third Division.
   Cavalry   Commissariat Train.
   Fourth Division   Fourth Division.

                    Rear Guard

The Divisions were composed as follows :—

Light Division (commanded by Sir George Brown), 7th, 19th, 23rd, 33rd, 77th, and 88th Regiments.

First Division (commanded by H.R.H. the Duke of Cambridge), the Grenadier Guards, Coldstream Guards, Scots Fusilier Guards, 42nd, 79th, and 93rd Highlanders.

Second Division (commanded by Sir De Lacy Evans), 30th, 41st, 47th, 49th, 55th, and 95th Regiments.

Third Division (commanded by Sir Richard England), 1st, 4th, 28th, 38th, 44th, and 50th Regiments.

Fourth Division (commanded by Sir George Cathcart), 20th, 21st, 46th, 57th, 63rd, 65th, and 1st Battalion of the Rifle Brigade.

Cavalry Division (commanded by Lord Lucan), 4th and 5th Dragoon Guards, 1st, 2nd, 4th, 6th, 8th, 13th, and 17th Dragoons, and 11th Hussars.

It was nine o'clock before the whole of the army was prepared to march, being delayed by the inadequate transport provided for the stores, baggage, etc. Many of our men fell down in the ranks, attacked by cholera, or from becoming faint and exhausted for want of water. If they recovered shortly, they followed us, with the rear guard; but if not, they were left to the tender mercies of any passer-by. It was certainly much to be lamented that we had no ambulance-wagons for these poor sick fellows, who fell out on the march; for had they been carried a mile or two, or had a drink of water, I have no doubt half of them would have rejoined their companies. Ambulance-carts ought surely to have attended each brigade, and each should have carried some medicine, particularly where the cholera was likely to affect the army. The medical officers in general carried a small bottle of brandy and flask of water, which they gave the men, and were thus enabled to do much good. Some of our poor fellows actually came to me, and on their knees besought me for a drink out of my flask; and I am happy to say that I managed to relieve a few of them. I found in our brigade that the men of the other regiments fell out almost ten to our one.

Our way led through dreary steppes, with long, irregular ridges of hills at intervals running down towards the sea. Curious thistles and long dry blades of grass abounded, and numerous hares fell victims to the advancing army, by running into the ranks, thus giving a little amusement to our fatigued men. Whenever the halt sounded, the men were ordered to lie down, and take off their packs.

About five p.m. we arrived at a rivulet called the Bulganac, to which the men rushed with great eagerness, and soon converted it into a stream of mud. I had to walk up, at a good pace, about a quarter of a mile, for clear water. Further up the stream could be seen a smoking village, which had been gutted and burnt by the Cossacks. The Imperial Post-house was situated close to the river, which was just twenty miles from Sebastopol. By this river we were to remain for the night. We found that there had been some skirmishing here an hour or two before, in which some horses had been killed and two or three men wounded.

After a short halt at the stream, the main body of the army had pushed on. The 8th, 11th, and 13th Light Dragoons were in front; and as about a mile in advance of the Post-house the

Cossacks were plainly seen on the hills beyond, skirmishers were thrown out by Lord Cardigan. The Cossacks advanced to meet them, their lances flashing in the sun. Lord Cardigan advanced to ascertain their strength; but finding that they had immense columns in reserve, he thought that our cavalry would be blown in ascending such a hill, and very likely surrounded and cut to pieces by a force three times their strength. He accordingly ordered them to halt, call in their skirmishers, and retire slowly. None of our artillery or infantry were near, not having topped the hills. When our skirmishers halted, the Russians commenced a sharp fire from their *videttes*, which, however, was quite harmless.

The cavalry then retired, every now and then facing about, to see if the Cossacks were preparing to charge. Shortly afterwards a round shot from the enemy's columns whizzed over their heads, and continuing its course, passed between the Rifle skirmishers, which were now advancing; and then another shot followed, which dropped into the midst of the 11th Hussars, killing a horse, and taking off his rider's legs; others also fell in their ranks, but it was astonishing how little harm they did.

Meanwhile Captain Maude's artillery came galloping up, but were halted by Lord Raglan, perhaps to entice the enemy to advance further. Our cavalry were drawn up, and after about twenty-five rounds from the enemy, our batteries opened. The practice of the Russian artillery was very good. Our shells were not so successful, except one, which, being better directed than the rest, fell into the midst of a column of Light Infantry, which were advanced to support the cavalry. Our fire was however soon so hot, that in twenty minutes the enemy retired. The French on our right had surprised some of the Russian cavalry, and opening some nine-pounders on them, they retired in great confusion. Our loss was about five or six horses killed and four men wounded, but the Russian loss must have been much more.

After the Russians had retired, the order came for our division to halt, and bivouac for the night. We could see the hills of Alma, about four miles distant, the scene of our next day's exploits. Our men commenced to gather the scorched weeds and thistles, to make fires to cook their rations, and all seemed delighted that this long, fatiguing day's march was over. I had scarcely washed myself in the stream, and swallowed some cold pork, when I was informed that I was to go, with two other officers and several men, on outlying picket, which was not a particularly pleasant duty after so hard a march in the broiling sun. The enemy were very near us, and we rather expected an attack. The night was very dark, and the fires in our camp shone bright and clear when I left it, as our picket post was at some little distance, and our sentries were thrown out all around the division, to ensure its safety and to guard against being surprised during the night. I went down for orders to Lord Raglan's quarters (the Imperial Post-house), and a very good house it was. Nearly everything had been taken out of it by the Russians, except a few bundles of herbs which hung in the kitchen, and a solitary peafowl, which was found at the door, and which I have no doubt afforded his Lordship a sumptuous supper.

I shall not easily forget my vain endeavours to find the bridge over the river in the dark, and walking up to my knees in the water. This little casualty did not, it may be imagined, tend to make me more comfortable for the night. Sleep was out of the question, for the sentries had to be visited every hour; and when the morning dawned, it found us wet through with the dew, which was heavier than I had ever before experienced.

Fortunately nothing occurred to prevent our men having a good night's rest; and at daybreak we drew in our sentries, and returned to the camp, where we found they had all finished their breakfasts, and were ready for a start. Many had died during the night. I was buckling my cloak on my pony, and had given up all idea of breakfast, when I espied a pot of coffee boiling on a fire, and found on approaching it that it belonged to the quartermaster sergeant, who immediately offered me a portion of it. I believe it saved my life, and I am sure he will say I was grateful for it. We all clad ourselves that morning as lightly as possible, and the ponies were in great requisition, for we expected to go into action very soon, but where we did not know. We were grieved to hear that poor Colonel Beckwith, of the Rifle Brigade, had been attacked with cholera during the night, I believe he was sent on board the *Orinoco,* and died shortly afterwards.

Chapter 5

The Battle of the Alma

Before daylight on the morning of the 20th of September we paraded in perfect silence, except the hum of five thousand voices, as there was not a drum or bugle to be heard in the camp. The troops remained under arms for about an hour, during which time the generals were employed in informing the brigadiers and commanding officers of the different regiments of the order of march. Our pioneers were employed by Sir George Cathcart in levelling the banks of the river Bulganac, to give a passage to the troops and artillery; and as soon as this was completed, we moved off. The French were on our extreme right, on the highroad near the sea, and the Turks acted as their reserve. It was known that the enemy had been busy in fortifying the heights beyond the river Alma, about four miles distant from the Bulganac, and that, as we had to cross that valley, they had resolved to resist our advance there, and try their strength with the Allied armies.

Our army was led by the Light and Second Divisions, followed by the First and Third, the Fourth acting as a reserve. We advanced in column, the leading division being perhaps a mile ahead of us; and as soon as we gained the summit of a ridge, we could plainly see the columns of the enemy crowning the hills beyond the Alma, and holding a position which gave them vast advantages over us. They had been actively engaged in preparing their lines of defence for three weeks, and in improving and fortifying to the utmost a position naturally very strong. The advance of our armies this day over the vast plain was a sight never to be forgotten by anyone who witnessed it: the forest of bayonets of the advancing columns glistened in the bright sun, the heat of which was tempered by a soft sea-breeze. The fleet also was to be seen about four miles distant, advancing with us, protecting our right, and the smoke of the steamers clouded the ocean. The army advanced in columns of brigades, its left being protected by cavalry and horse artillery, covering an area of five or six miles.

At about one p.m. the English Light Division came in sight of the village of Burliuk, and the French Light Division that of Almatamak, both being situated on the right bank of the river Alma, a small winding stream with high banks, in most places about knee-deep, though very frequently with pools and eddies which are unfordable. There were many trees and small hamlets on the right bank, with gardens and vineyards attached to them; but they were all gutted and in flames when we arrived, and a number of the trees were thrown down by the Russians, to impede us in our course. Here and there could be seen bundles of straw, fastened on poles, at which no doubt their artillery had been practising and getting the range of their guns.

On the north or right side of the river the country is very level, sloping down within three hundred yards of the water, and at a quarter of a mile distant the stream is not visible, but its situation must be guessed at by the trees and shrubs, which only grow in the valley at the water's edge. On the south side of the river, which the enemy occupied, it is very different; ravines, formed by the winter's torrents and commanded by the shelving heights above, run in all directions. On the highest of these rested the strength of the Russian position, and their guns commanded the whole valley, far beyond the ridge on the opposite side, to a distance of fourteen or fifteen hundred yards. A curious ridge of mountain runs along the river's course, varying in height from five to eight hundred feet, and appearing like cliffs as you approach the sea. On the summit of these the Russians had erected earthwork batteries, containing 24 and 32-

pounders, which were supported by field-pieces and howitzers; and lines of skirmishers were planted on the sides, armed with two-groove rifles, carrying a solid conical ball seven or eight hundred yards. It was these that did so much damage to the French, keeping up a brisk fire the whole time. In their first battery were thirteen 32-pounders, brass guns, of excellent quality, and in their other batteries about twenty-five guns in all.

The first intimation of an attack was from the steamers, which, getting in close to the land, commenced shelling the Russians at 12.30 a.m. Their fire lasted an hour and a half, and their practice was very good; so good, indeed, that they succeeded in driving the enemy back 2500 yards from the sea, receiving no damage themselves from the batteries. During this time the French were scaling the heights, which were considered impregnable by Menschikoff, and therefore ill protected either by troops or batteries; but the Zouaves were seen creeping up like goats, and before long formed on the summit, before the enemy's guns were brought to bear on them. Canrobert's Division then came up to their support.

The Turks were with Marshal St. Arnaud's portion of the army, which had no active part in the struggle assigned to them. About one o'clock a host of skirmishers were seen ascending the hill and keeping up a heavy fire, covering the advance of masses of French troops which were behind them. Now the battle commenced in real earnest, and before long the heavy guns of the Russians (32's and 24's) pealed forth their awful thunder from all sides, mingled with our smaller guns (9's), and volleys of musketry from the Russian and French skirmishers. Ours were also advancing, and when within eighteen hundred yards, the shots were seen ploughing up the ground between our riflemen, and continuing their course, dropped into the columns some little distance in the rear. Dense volumes of smoke came sweeping up the valley from the villages and hamlets which the Russians had set on fire, and it was very difficult to discern what was going on. This annoyed and interrupted us much. Our troops halted, and when they came near the village, and lay down within range of the batteries, these opened a tremendous fire on our lines. This, however, only served to madden our men, and make them more determined.

The French had crossed the Alma on the right, and the time was fast drawing near for the British to attack. Though the infantry were passive, our artillery were actively employed in shelling the Russians, their shots taking great effect; but what could our little 9-pounders be expected to do against the heavy guns of the enemy? They, however, did their duty, and that right well.

The moment had now arrived for our army to advance, and Lord Raglan, looking round and seeing a brave army by his side on whom he could depend, gave the order for the whole line to advance. They did advance, dashing like fiends through the river. The vineyards by the stream were full of Russian riflemen, who kept up a heavy fire on our troops, and the grape and canister-shot, together with a heavy fire of musketry which fell amongst them, mowed them down by hundreds. Now commenced one of the most bloody actions in the annals of war; but England's blood was up and boiling, and the men showed that bulldog courage which no other nation in the whole world possesses, during one of the warmest fires ever known.

Sir George Brown, on his grey horse, was to be seen leading on the Light Division to victory. The Second Division, headed by Sir De Lacy Evans in person, dashed at the crowded heights. The 7th Fusiliers, led by Colonel Yea, were swept down by twenties; but this was no time for a roll-call. Brigadier-General Pennefather, with the 30th, 55th, and 95th by his side, was to be seen cheering on his men, and rolls of musketry pealed from their advancing lines. The 41st, 47th, and 49th, under Brigadier-General Adams, bravely charged on, in the thick of battle. The 7th, greatly reduced, halted to rally for a few moments, and the officers and men of the 23rd, 15th, 33rd, 88th, and 77th were falling by fifties.

Sir George Brown's old grey at last fell, but the gallant general, jumping up in an instant, shouted, "23rd, I am all right,—be sure I'll remember this day," and led them on again, as if nothing had happened. The Guards and Highlanders were storming the heights on the left, and were falling by dozens, when an immense mass of Russian infantry were seen moving down towards the battery. Against these a couple of guns were soon directed, upon which they retired in great confusion, after six or seven shots, leaving complete lines of dead behind them. This greatly relieved our infantry, and they continued their progress up the hill.

It is said that Sir Colin Campbell thus addressed his splendid brigade just before they charged:—"Highlanders, I am going to ask of you a favour; it is, that you will act so as to justify me in asking permission of the Queen for you to wear the bonnet!" They well obeyed Sir Colin's wishes in this charge. Their gallant leader had his horse killed under him; but he was soon on his feet again, and at their head, shouting, "We'll hae nane but Highland bonnets here!"

The Guards, with the Duke of Cambridge, coming on at the same time, together with the 83rd, claimed the honour of taking a gun: they stormed the right of the battery, and the Highlanders the left. The Second and Light Divisions were on the heights, having suffered a great loss. Eight of the 23rd R. W. Fusiliers' officers fell here. Poor Lieutenant-Colonel Chester was shot, I believe, waving, one of the colours which he had taken when Anstruther was killed, and falling backwards, was caught by his servant, who took him on his back, and was carrying him to the rear, when another shot struck him and proved fatal. Captain Wynn was shot through the eye, almost at the muzzle of one of the enemy's guns. Sir William Young was shot whilst his regiment was retiring a little to rally, and he was found dead when they advanced again. Delmé Radcliffe was shot through the mouth, and Evans and the others lay at no great distance from one another.

I deeply deplored the loss of so many I had known intimately. Some of the officers told me that the most harassing part they had to perform was lying down in line before they advanced, when the grape and canister shot fell into their ranks like hailstones, and swept many of them away. The Russians seem always to aim at the officers, most particularly at those with the colours; and certainly, with their gold lace, they are nothing more than good targets for them.

The French had the guns turned on the enemy, who were flying in great confusion and perfectly panic-stricken, though covered by their cavalry, which were in great strength. They left behind them three generals, three cannons, between six and seven hundred prisoners, and about four thousand killed and wounded on the field.

Thus ended this frightful bloodshed; and although we gained the day, we felt as if there was something left undone. Where was our cavalry, to follow up the retreating army, and take their cannon from them and prisoners? We had plenty, but not where they were wanted. But, weak as they were, the Russian cavalry never gave them a chance to charge or meet them in the whole engagement. The number of our troops actually engaged with the enemy were about 14,000, for two divisions scarcely fired a shot. To these were opposed 20,000 Russians, together with 20,000 more engaged with the French, who behaved most gallantly. Numerous spectators had come out of Sebastopol, having been assured by Menschikoff that they would be quite safe, and that it would be a fine sight to see the Allies peppered for three weeks; for that period, according to a despatch to the Emperor found in his carriage, he expected to hold his position. How surprised he and his friends must have been to find themselves fairly put to flight in as many hours! The English had 1500 men put *hors de combat,* and the French about 1200, the field of battle being covered with the dead and dying.

Shortly afterwards Lord Raglan published the following General Order:—

> The Commander of the Forces congratulates the troops on the brilliant success that attended their unrivalled efforts in the battle of the 20th instant, on which occasion they carried a most formidable position, defended by large masses of Russian infantry, and a most powerful and nu-

merous artillery. Their conduct was in unison with that of our gallant Allies, whose spirited and successful attack of the left of the heights occupied by the enemy, cannot fail to have attracted their notice and admiration.

The Commander of the Forces thanks the army most warmly for its gallant exertions. He witnessed them with pride and satisfaction; and it will be his pleasing duty to report, for the Queen's information, how well they have earned Her Majesty's approbation, and how gloriously they maintained the honour of the British name.

Lord Raglan condoles most sincerely with the troops on the loss of so many gallant officers and brave men, whose memory it will be a consolation to their friends to feel will ever be cherished in the annals of our army.

(Signed) J. B. B. Estcourt.

A general officer who had been taken prisoner, asked where we were going, reported Sebastopol to be very strongly fortified, and said we should require more than our force to take it. His excuse for the Russians not holding Alma longer than they did was that "they expected to meet men, not devils."

At dusk the Fourth Division moved down from the heights, and halted at a place not far from the river which had been a Russian encampment, a most putrid, filthy place. The dew and fog were very heavy, and our prospects for the night by no means cheering; but we soon made a sort of hut with our waterproof coats, not unlike a badly-built dog-kennel, and having rolled ourselves up two or three together in our blankets, we slept for some hours very soundly. An hour before daylight we stood to our arms, and moved up again to the heights. We were in great hopes that we should leave this ground altogether; but were told to remain until the dead were buried, and the wounded sent on board the ships, which were lying off the mouth of the river.

This day was employed in placing the dead bodies in rows, and counting them previous to their being buried in large pits. Several of them were buried in the batteries where they fell, being laid in the ditch and covered with earth. The dead and wounded Russians were lying in all directions, and our men rifled their pockets; but strange to say, the Russian soldiers generally keep their money in their boots, where a piece of gold was frequently found, which made us suppose that they had received their pay not long before. I heard that some of our men had got as much as £20 value by robbing the dead.

The English soldiers fired off and broke up the muskets which the Russians had thrown down in their flight, and shot the poor wounded horses which were lying in all directions. Arms and accoutrements were strewn about everywhere. Our soldiers used the barrels of the firelocks as pokers, and one foolish fellow putting the breech of a loaded musket into the fire, was shot through the leg.

The wounded Russians received the greatest kindness from our men, who gave them water, biscuits, and everything they possessed. They even lent them their pipes, for which they generally were most grateful. Sometimes, however, these kindnesses were offered to men who, though in great agony, refused with a sullen shake of the head to accept them. These were dangerous fellows; and I believe it is too true that one of our men was fired at by a man to whom he had offered some water. The body of a poor Russian officer was lying near our camp; he had two medals and a miniature of a lady in his pocket. He had evidently been killed by a shell, as his head was dreadfully disfigured. I thought the Russian private soldiers, with very few exceptions, ugly-looking fellows, and they almost all seemed to me to have fat, pale faces, devoid of intellectual expression.

Near the river we saw some of the ovens in which had been baked the coarse black bread on which the Russian army seems principally to subsist.

We here heard that the enemy was retreating as quickly as possible to Sebastopol, and was then between the rivers Katcha and Belbeck. As these were very formidable positions, we fully expected that they would have opposed us at one of them; but having put such entire confidence in their position at Alma (which they evidently thought was impregnable), they did not think it necessary to make a second line of defence, and were too much cowed by their defeat to make so speedily another stand. Rather a strong body of Cossacks was seen at some little distance from us in the country to our left; but they did not attempt to attack us, nor had we the slightest apprehension that they would do so. They were evidently sent to watch our movements at a respectful distance.

On the 22nd the weather became very much warmer. For many hours of the day the sun was scorching, and there was not a tree or shade of any kind to protect us from its rays. Although strong parties of our men were occupied on the previous day in burying the dead, there still remained a great number unburied. The sight was sad and sickening, and the very air seemed to be already tainted; indeed many of our officers on duty returned quite sick and ill from the field. Numbers of men and officers went down to bathe in the river, and many of the men took the opportunity of washing their shirts. I went up the stream with some of my brother officers, and we had a most refreshing bath. The river is not broad, but very meandering and pretty, and reminded me very much of an English trout-stream. Willow-trees here and there dipped into the water, and in their boughs were a number of magpies, chattering and making a fearful noise as they flew from tree to tree.

On our return to the field we found the men breaking up the Russian fire-arms. This caused no slight danger to the bystanders and themselves, for many of the muskets were loaded, and the concussion caused them to go off; many bullets whistled unpleasantly near our heads. I examined carefully many of these arms. They were remarkably clean and quite free from rust, though there was no symptom of oil having been used about them; the barrels were very long, made of polished iron, and fastened to the stock by bands of brass. The bayonets were easily broken, being very slight and soft. I thought these muskets remarkably top-heavy, and not nearly so handy or portable as ours, though in reality much lighter. The stocks are small, though clumsy, made of very bad wood, and we found a great number of them broken. I should be very sorry to fire one of them off, for it appeared to me that few of them would be likely to stand proof. The powder was coarse, but appeared clean and unadulterated, and the cartridges were very neatly made. Their rifles are very far superior to their muskets, and carry a conical ball, which has two projecting grooves.

The enemy were particularly careful not to display any colours on the 20th, for fear, I suppose, of losing them. I heard that the first of our guns which was brought on the heights was loaded and fired by its own officers at the retreating army, and I was told that Colonel Dacres was one of them.

The wretched duty of burying the dead was completed on the 22nd, and the wounded were carried in litters on board the ships. The sailors were again very busy, and did their very utmost to relieve the poor sufferers. They had a capital contrivance by which they carried the wounded very comfortably;—a hammock fastened to an oar, in which they slung those who were most helpless.

It would be impossible to describe or to praise sufficiently the untiring exertions of our medical men, who worked day and night with almost superhuman endurance, endeavouring to save life. All possible credit is due to them for their devotion to these terrible duties. I heard of three successful amputations of the leg at the hip-joint having been performed by Dr. Alexander. He was the principal medical officer of the Light Division, who had, as I heard, more than a thousand cases for surgical treatment. Never was there a more terrible scene than the hospital presented.

The instances of individual daring during the battle of the Alma are almost too numerous to attempt to narrate. One brave fellow of the 7th Fusiliers, rushing out to the front, bayoneted two Russians in their leading column. Poor Captain Monck, of the same corps, killed one man with his sword, and knocked down another with his fist, who was in the act of shooting him; but, poor fellow! he was himself shot immediately afterwards. Soon after the battle several men came into the camp, and gave themselves up as prisoners. They stated that they belonged to the army of Moldavia, and that they had not long been in the Crimea.

We lost many men from cholera during the night of the 22nd. It was heart-rending to hear the groans of the poor fellows. They however had every comfort which under the circumstances could be afforded them; they were brought to a fire and their legs rubbed by orderlies; indeed, the medical officers paid them every possible attention.

CHAPTER 6

The Black River

Orders were received late at night to hold ourselves in readiness to march on the following day; and heartily glad were we to leave the bloody field of Alma at daylight. All was stir and bustle with us, and the drums and bugles of the French announced that they also were on the move. Our teeth chattered with cold when we awoke, the dew having wetted us a good deal, and it was some time before circulation was restored. I found a cup of coffee, as on many other occasions, an excellent restorative; indeed I never felt well or fit for work until I had taken one. It always seemed to put new life into me, and to be the best antidote to the damp, dewy air and rising exhalations.

It was a bright sunny morning when we left these dreary scenes, and the advance sounded by the French bugle was cheering to our ears. There was no delay, and the whole allied army was quickly on the move. We were compelled to leave many wounded Russians on the field, but not until their wounds had been dressed, and we had done all in our power to alleviate their sufferings. An English surgeon, Dr. Thomson, of the 44th, and his servant, remained, by order of Lord Raglan. This sad duty was most nobly and efficiently performed, as far as their physical power under the circumstances enabled them; but the difficulties of their task were greater than any two human beings could surmount. There they were, in that dreary field of death and misery, without a friend, and with no food, except a little salt meat and biscuit. It was explained to a Russian officer among the wounded, that Dr. Thomson was left to perform this duty, and that he ought to be protected. Dr. Thomson was also told to hoist a flag of truce if the Cossacks or any armed parties came there.

The country through which we now marched was very barren and hilly; no large trees, but here and there a few patches of oak saplings met the eye. Winding through these hills ran the high-road to Sebastopol, which was here nothing more than a beaten track. A great number of helmets, knapsacks, and other accoutrements, which had evidently been thrown off by many of the routed army in order to accelerate their flight, were to be seen strewn about in all directions; also the carcases of horses, in a filthy state of putrefaction. Now and then we halted to allow the wagon-train to come up, and in order to rest the men, although we did not march much more than two miles an hour.

In the afternoon we arrived at the lovely valley through which flows the rapid little river Katcha. It winds towards the sea amidst beautiful gardens and luxuriant vineyards. Villas and hamlets, with their pretty gardens and lawns, are dotted along the river-side. The rural village of Eskel, on the left bank, was entirely deserted, but we found a little hay and grain for our horses. One of the stories in circulation was, that the Russian army was retreating from Sebastopol, together with its inhabitants, and that we had nothing to do but to march in and take the place. As soon as our men had piled their arms, and we had received orders to bivouac for the night, I, with some other officers, proceeded to the river, and refreshed ourselves with a delicious bath.

We passed through beautiful vineyards, where hung large clusters of the finest black grapes I ever saw. I do not believe that they are injurious, if the skins and stones be thrown away; but our men, when they first entered the vineyards, despised this precaution, which they found to their cost to be necessary. The hay-lofts in the village were filled with soldiers hunting for hens' nests, and I met several men who seemed to have been successful, their caps being full of eggs. I was much amused by seeing an old hen coursed by three stout grenadiers, who seemed most intent on her destruction,

The men thoroughly enjoyed this place. It was such a change for them after the hardships they had undergone, and the dreadful scene of carnage which they had so lately witnessed. Some were to be seen with looking-glasses and pictures on their heads, which they had found in some of the houses; indeed they appeared to take a particular fancy to the furniture. I saw many soldiers running off with chairs, small tables, etc., whether to sit on, or to use as firewood, it was not easy to discover. Everything in the houses betokened the speedy departure of their inmates, and signs of the progress of a devastating army were sadly apparent. Chairs and tables were upset in all directions, pillows and mattresses cut to pieces, and the windows broken. It was evident that the Cossacks had been there, and that they had done all possible injury in their progress, but I fear our army was not very slow in following their example. Some of the houses had pretty verandas, covered with roses and clematis. The gardens were full of apples and delicious pears, and I saw a few apricots. There were many wine-presses in the village.

A deserter came in to us during the evening and told us that there were many Tartars in the neighbourhood, concealed in the bushes. He was immediately despatched to tell them that if they returned to their village they would be protected. Shortly afterwards a number of ugly fellows made their appearance, and naturally enough were not a little surprised and dismayed at what had taken place in their humble abodes. We discovered that the Russians had halted here on the night after the battle of the Alma; but an alarm being given in the middle of the night, that the Allies were advancing, they fled in great confusion in all directions; some to Sebastopol, others to Bakshiserai, etc. Several sentries were planted, in order to protect property as much as possible; but it is no easy task to stop the ravages of a victorious army. The Greek church was especially guarded, in order to prevent its being pillaged.

The First, Third, and Light Divisions bivouacked on the

heights above the Katcha, and the Second and Fourth on the side of the hill close to the river. After dinner we turned in for the night, refreshed by our bath and much pleased with our quarters, which were much more comfortable than any we had had for some time, and we all enjoyed the blessing of a long, uninterrupted night's rest. Our pony seemed to enjoy himself as much as we did, and fared well on some capital hay and corn, which our servants procured for him.

The next morning (24th) we prepared for a move, but there was a long delay, and the troops were much fatigued by remaining in the baking sun. This delay was, however, unavoidable. We were very glad to hear of the arrival of the 57th, and our brigadier-general, Goldie, also that the Scots Greys were being landed from the *Himalaya*. The French also had received reinforcements, amounting to 9000 men. The landing of these took an unusually long time, and there were many sick to send to the ships; but the fleet, which was lying off the mouth of the river, rendered every possible assistance.

Our march this day was to the Belbeck, a distance of five or six miles, through an undulating country. The valley of the Belbeck is on a much grander scale than the valley which I have just attempted to describe. The right side is very barren and rugged, and deep ravines run down to the river; but the left is very different, being much wooded with trees of small size. The winding road to Sebastopol skirts this hill. When we arrived at the summit we could plainly see the houses in this beautifully situated city, and all eyes and glasses were anxiously directed towards it. We were about four miles from it, and the intervening country was covered with trees and brushwood, very different from what we had hitherto seen.

Hearing that the enemy were in position on the right, we made a flank movement to the left, crossing the river at the village of Belbeck, and from a sign-post which we saw at a post-house, found that we were on the high-road to Sebastopol. By this movement we flanked the batteries, and compelled the enemy to retreat and withdraw their guns. The road in the valley was so full of dust that we were almost choked; the sun was broiling, and there was not a breath of wind; the artillery passing at the same time as ourselves.

We crossed a wide bridge, by the side of which was a ford. The horses being taken out of the guns, were led down to the stream, which was full of oxen and mules quenching their thirst, and two or three officers on their chargers, to say nothing of lines of soldiers all along the water's edge. We were then marched into a meadow by the river. Here we got out of the dust, and a long row of willows protected us from the sun. This was the most verdant place we had seen since landing, and our ponies enjoyed the nibble at the fresh grass, having had nothing but dried stuff, which they snatched at intervals on the plain. Here our men piled their arms and roamed about, some picking fruit in the excellent gardens with which the valley abounded, and others luxuriating by the little stream which glided through it.

The French artillery now came by us at a tremendous pace, charging up the road on the hill on the left side of the river. I was much amused at the indifference a driver on one of the leaders showed when his companion on a wheeler was jolted off. He did not attempt to stop, but allowed him to overtake him as best he could, laughing heartily all the time; but it was no joke to the poor fellow, who was very nearly run over by the gun-wheel.

Towards the evening we were moved up to the hill on the left, and were ordered to bivouac for the night amongst some small oak-trees at the side of the Sebastopol road. The French were on the hill above us, and our different divisions all around, but the head-quarters and commissariat remained in the village, a mile below us. The whole wood was soon seen in motion, and the cracking of the boughs and the rising smoke showed us that we should soon have our coffee and dinner. Ponies were passing down the road to the river, laden with water-kegs slung round their heads, tails, or any convenient place. With two other officers, I commenced cutting boughs for our hut, and soon got a very good one constructed. At an early hour we turned in, expecting to have a good night's rest; but were aroused at night by perpetual disturbance. At an early hour an alarm also was raised by some wretched camp followers, one of whom came charging our hut, catching his toe in the roof and levelling the whole to the ground. We expected at least to find a Cossack standing before us, but no one was to be found. The greatest confusion prevailed: men stood to their arms, ponies were saddled, and every preparation made for an immediate attack. It was, however, discovered that this excitement had all been occasioned by a few loose horses galloping about. This confusion over, we began to repair damages, which took some little time in the dark.

But this was not all. At two o'clock in the morning we were again aroused by a gun, and by some small arms going off. Out we went again, and stood to our arms; but as we were obliged to enter our house head first, we had to get out heels first, and as there were three of us, and all in rather a hurry, down came our kennel again. We played the same part over again, and were again aroused by these invisible Cossacks at five a.m. The only difference in the last alarm was that we did not consider it worthwhile to mend our abode again, but packing it up, cooked our breakfasts, haying passed a wretched night.

The firing during the night we now, discovered had proceeded from the outposts of the French, who seeing some Cossacks in front, gave them a volley and a shot from a six-pounder, which soon scattered them in all directions. It was a great nuisance to us to be roused by such noises, then uncommon, but we soon afterwards got used to them.

Preparations were now made by us for our march, which were attended with great excitement, for we fully expected to be in Sebastopol the following day. Such was our idea of the place and our own power. We supposed that the French were to attack the forts on the north side of the harbour, and that we were to attack the town on the south side. In the midst of our enthusiasm we received orders to return with the 68th Regiment to protect the sick, who had been sent off to the ships, lying at the mouth of the river, and we took up our position in line on the side of the hill, in an open space overlooking the valley.

It is impossible to imagine a much more delightful place, or to see greater luxuriance or more abundant vegetation than we now saw around us; there is a constant succession of gardens, small houses, lawns, and charming little villas. I observed with my glass, in a most picturesque spot, shaded by lofty and widespreading trees, a monument railed round, apparently the tomb of some grandee. The whole place was lined with poplar-trees.

The Scots Greys now came up the hill, and a finer or better-horsed regiment it is impossible to imagine; strong, healthy fellows, fresh from England, and noble horses, in the best condition; so soon, alas! to change, and too many of them to meet a soldier's death. The colonel was mounted on the finest animal I ever saw. We ascertained that we were to bivouac in our present position that night, and accordingly made all preparations. It was very amusing to watch the steamers, which were keeping up a brisk cannonade, and shelling the farts on the north side of Sebastopol. Their practice was at very long range, so that they did not much damage them; but they succeeded in drawing the attention of the Russians from the great flank march to the south-east, which had now commenced by the main body of the army. We wore left behind in a most unpleasant position; and had the enemy come out in force, we must have been cut to pieces. That fine general, Sir George Cathcart, seemed well aware of our danger, for he remained on the alert the whole night, and rode about to visit our pickets, etc.

The other division of the army commenced a march which history will probably relate as one of the boldest movements ever made in the face of an enemy. The reason assigned for it was, that the generals had discovered that the enemy had thrown up batteries on the north side of the harbour of Sebastopol, which, in conjunction with Fort Constantine and the Star Fort, would cause us severe loss, if we should attempt to attack the town in this quarter. It was, therefore, considered advisable to make a flank movement on Balaklava, by which we should avoid these batteries, render them useless, and find the weakest side of Sebastopol laid open to us.

The march now lay in the direction of the Black River, through a thickly-wooded country, intersected with numerous roads, not broad enough to permit our men to march more than four deep. The army was consequently much scattered, and in some disorder, and had the enemy then attacked us they must have inflicted upon us a severe blow and loss; but they did not possess courage to do this after their recent defeat, and made no attempt to impede our progress. K—— went on picket, and we happily remained undisturbed that night, and on the next morning at an early hour we followed the advancing column of the Allied army.

In the bushes by the roadside lay many dead and dying, who had suffered from the chill of the night, the morning dew, and the broiling sun. A wounded Turk, with folded arms, which clasped his firelock, gazed at us with ghastly countenance, whereon was written agony; and the groans of those still unrelieved by death came piercingly into our ears. What assistance could we render? The cry of the physicians was, "We have no physic for them." The road was strewed with shakos, those maddening, sun-attracting portions of the soldier's dress, which crush their very brains. *Minié* balls and other bullets lay about, indicative of some sharp work recently: they had cut off boughs and barked some trees in their course. At intervals could be seen the white houses of Sebastopol, with their sparkling windows.

Lord Raglan had a narrow escape in the march through the wood this day. He was some distance in front, when suddenly, in an opening of the wood, he came upon a body of Russian infantry. They were but a few hundred yards from him, and turned out to be the baggage-guard of a large body of Russians who were on the march from Sebastopol to Bakshiserai. Lord Raglan immediately rode back in rear of the First Division artillery. The cavalry, consisting of the 8th and 11th Hussars, were quickly sent out, and the guns brought to bear on the astonished convoy. The Rifles, in skirmishing order, kept up a heavy fire on them, and the cavalry making a charge, they were completely routed, leaving behind them an immense quantity of baggage for two miles in the direction of their flight. This was lawful plunder, and the soldiers were allowed to break open the carts and help themselves, under the superintendence of an officer, to prevent squabbling. Wearing apparel of all descriptions was found in great abundance, together with dressing-cases, jewellery, ornaments, and wine, and I heard that some specie was also taken. Fine large cloaks, lined with fur, and some hussar jackets, covered with lace, were also seized and sold by the soldiers. Menschikoff's carriage likewise was taken, and Captain Feel, R.N., was lucky enough to get his Grand Orders as a Prince of Russia. This put our men in the highest possible spirits, and enlivened their long, dusty march to the Black River, where they halted and bivouacked for the night.

The little skirmish and capture of the baggage on the 25th accounted for the bullets we saw on the road on the following day. The men of the Fourth Division suffered much for want of water, for it was a sultry day, and almost suffocating in the woods, where there was not a breath of air. When we arrived at Mackenzie's farm we found that the wells had been rendered useless by the Cossacks: one was filled up with stones, and the other was said to be poisoned. The farm-house was a long, barrack-looking place, having been used as a guard-house for a plantation which had been made there for the Russian navy by an old Russian admiral of the name of Mackenzie, of Scottish origin. We remained here for some time, in a large open space, which was also partly occupied by French troops, nearly broiled by the sun and smothered with dust; but after some little time a spring was discovered at no great distance, and our men were greatly relieved. I however fancied that this might have been chemically prepared by the enemy, and K—— and I contented ourselves with a pull at the flask which hung by my side.

We were now startled by a loud report and volume of smoke close to us, and found that our people were blowing up some Russian tumbrils which they had left behind.

It was late in the day when we moved off towards the Black River, where we were to halt for the night. A very rough winding road, cut on the side of the mountain, led us into the valley. The dust on this road was beyond all conception, caused by the late great traffic and the soft stone of which it was made. Heaps of powder from the enemy's tumbrils lay in all directions; the wagons themselves being pitched over the bank were stuck in the trees several yards below. In the middle of the road lay a dead Russian, not a soldier, a prey for the vultures and wolves, in which this country abounds. When we arrived in the valley we were in open country, with steep mountains on either side of us, topped with brushwood; and now and then a mined building struck the eye. An hour before sunset we arrived at the Black River, and just as we had taken up our position for the night we were alarmed by the cry, "Here they come!" Seeing numbers of soldiers rushing to their respective corps, both French and English, our gallant commander immediately faced us in the direction of the as yet invisible enemy, and prepared for an attack. But it turned out that our men and the French had wandered up on the hills to some village gardens, and the Tartars had come out and chased them with broomsticks, in a most successful manner. The retreat of a fat officer amused us much.

We heard that Lord Raglan had left this place in the morning, and had pushed on to Balaklava, which place, together with its garrison, had surrendered. Lord Raglan and his staff were the first to advance towards the town, not anticipating any resistance, until they were astonished by a shell or two dropping amongst them from the old Genoese Forts above. These places appeared to be nothing but ruins; but it was now discovered that a small body of Russians were here, with their governor, who intended to defend the place. Their cannonade was responded to by the *Agamemnon* outside, which sent some shells rattling against the ruins, giving them soon a very dilapidated appearance. The Rifles, and a part of the Light Division, then advanced, and opened fire at seven hundred yards, gradually closing on the fort. This obliged them to hang out a flag of truce and surrender. They were all made prisoners; and the governor, upon being asked why he had fired from a place which he must have been aware he could not hold, replied that he considered himself bound to do so, until compelled to surrender. The shells were projected from small brass mortars. The prisoners were sent off to Constantinople. Shortly afterwards an English steamer came into the harbour, and the inhabitants showed every symptom of friendship, bringing out fruit and flowers to Lord Raglan, who promised them his protection.

The Commander-in-chief took up his head-quarters in some of the best houses in the place, and in the afternoon the monster hull of the *Agamemnon* was seen, as it were, being launched out of the mountains. It then entered this great pond and anchored in the centre, and Sir Edmund Lyons was very shortly seen coming ashore to pay a visit to Lord Raglan. The *Diamond* and *Caradoc* also came in, together with another steamer, the *Hydaspes*. It is an extraordinary place; in feet, a regular basin, the sea not being visible from it. It is about half a mile in length, and varies from one hundred and fifty to two hundred and fifty yards in breadth. The shores are barren, rocky, and precipitous, and overlap one another at the entrance, rendering it invisible from the sea. The village is a very miserable fishing town; and outside the harbour many nets were seen when the fleet first arrived, which were hung on their fishing stakes under the rocks. These were, however, soon taken away by the sailors. About two hundred feet overhead were the Genoese Forts in total ruin, which had not been improved by the *Agamemnon* shells; but the bastions, walls, and towers were still visible. The town is approached from the open country and valley, through a narrow pass between two mountains, which might have proved formidable if only disputed by a small force possessed of the slightest enterprise.

Lord Raglan had now secured his base for operations, the army and navy having been once more united.

CHAPTER 7

Balaklava

The following morning at daylight (26th September) the Fourth Division was on the move, and crossing the Black River by a substantial well-built bridge, we came to a halt on the side of the road, to allow a French division to move on ahead of us, as well as our commissariat-carts, ammunition, etc. We were highly pleased at the sight of about fifty French ambulance mules laden with sick: some of the poor fellows were sitting up, others reclining in a kind of folding chair, lashed on either side of the animals, which were remarkably fine and powerful, carrying two men each on their backs. Each mule had an attendant or muleteer who guided it, particularly over rough ground, where they went in the easiest and most careful manner, picking their road like cats.

On two or three I saw English soldiers. The poor fellows on their backs seemed very comfortable, quite different from the Turkish invalids who followed just after, in wretched, rough, creaking *arabas*, drawn by clumsy oxen, and who looked as if they would die at every jolt, or have their heads shaken off. When they had all passed by we moved on slowly towards Balaklava, and General Canrobert rode along our line. He was greeted by a hearty cheer, at which he looked highly gratified. He is a fine, soldier-like looking fellow, having his arm in a sling from a wound he received at Alma. He was followed by a large escort, principally of *spahis*, and our men had their usual laugh at the "old women," as they called them in joke. A long line of French skirmishers, consisting of those active fellows, the *Chasseurs de Vincennes,* came sweeping across the plain, passing through our line, and finding more hares than Russians in the long dry grass.

At length we entered a long valley, at the bottom of which could be seen the town and harbour of Balaklava, full of our noble ships. Several of these had come in that day, and were busily engaged in disembarking their monster guns belonging to the heavy artillery and siege train. These were fifty in number, composed of 32- and 64-pounders, together with Lancaster guns, which throw a solid 90-pound shot. We placed great reliance in the latter, having heard so much of their wonderful range. Scattered houses extended some little way up the valley towards us. We were not, however, to halt here, but, taking a sweep, wheeled round to our right, and got into the Sebastopol road.

When we had gained the heights, we could plainly see the sea; and we passed some deserted farm-houses which had stacks of hay and straw in the yards. Our line of march now took us over an undulating plain, without a tree, except an occasional orchard and a few poplars. Some of the men were actively employed in sucking pieces of honeycomb from beehives which they had knocked over in the valley we had just left. Soon, however, all eyes were intently gazing in that quarter where Sebastopol was expected to be seen. At last we came to a halt, and walking on a few yards to the edge of the ridge, we saw the domes and batteries of this wonderful city before us, standing out in bold relief from the dark blue sea beyond. It did not strike us as being a fine city; for only a few good houses or buildings are to be seen from where we were on the south side.

We now took a turn to the right, being about two miles and a half from Sebastopol, and crossed a valley where was a deserted market-gardener's cottage, surrounded by a fine garden. This was soon full of soldiers, who helped themselves to fruit and vegetables of the choicest description.

General T——, however, made his appearance, and ordered them out. An amateur friend of ours, however, in his cap and shooting-jacket, remained until the last, busily employed in filling his pockets with carrots and onions for his dinner. Observing him, the general, with a voice of thunder, pealed forth, "Whose servant are you, Sir? If you don't come out immediately, I'll send you to the provost-marshal and have you flogged."

Our friend, as you may imagine, looked rather astonished at this, and went up to the general, when an explanation took place. They laughed heartily at the mistake, and we were not a little amused at the speedy absolution which was given to the culprit.

An excellent spring was found close by, which supplied the town with water, and the men soon quenched their thirst, and filled the water-kegs (with which they were all supplied) from it. We had not advanced much further before we came to a quarry on the brow of a hill, which was covered with brushwood and oak saplings. Sebastopol was plainly to be seen from this point, about two miles distant, and the Russians in great numbers were observed to be hard at work at their mud-batteries, which they had just commenced, this side of the town being unfortified. I fancy that our appearance in this quarter was the last thing they contemplated.

It was decided that we were to bivouac here for the night. A small stone house, which had probably been occupied by the quarry-labourers, was set apart for Sir George Cathcart; but he kindly gave it up to the sick of the division, and had his own little picket-tent, with table outside, pitched in a prominent position, and the Fourth Division flag was planted on the roof of the house. Our artillery were drawn up close to us; the guns, unlimbered, faced the town, and the horses remained saddled all night. These precautions were highly necessary, as the Fourth Division was the only one here, the Second Division being about two miles distant, and our number not exceeding 5000 men. We were, however, consoled when our general was heard to say, that he could hold our position against 80,000 Russians. Such was the contempt he entertained for them.

Our regiment was formed in column, and I soon saw my

companion, K——, with a huge log as big as himself on his shoulders, which he had found in the quarries. He insisted on my splitting it up, which, without an axe, was rather a difficult proceeding, and in fact could not be accomplished, but we kept shoving the end into the fire until we turned in for the night. Shortly afterwards, I heard a wretched chicken chirping in the bushes close to my ear; whereupon a hunt ensued, but the miserable little animal made its escape. Having cut a hole in the bushes, and put our feet to the fire, we turned in, and a wretched cold night we had, for one blanket between two is not much when the dew begins to fall on it. K—— had none, but I was too glad to share mine with him.

A sounder sleeper I never saw, nor a more noisy one, for he (snored frightfully; and having only one pillow (my saddle-bags, made of hard leather), it frequently sounded like volleys of musketry in my ear, and woke me up with a start. However, a better or more cheerful companion I never met. Often, when he saw my thoughts were too long wandering to scenes far away, he gave me a "view halloo" in my ear, or a dig in my ribs, and then with joyous laugh and merriment dispelled, for the time, the clouds which were gathering on my mind. Several men were taken ill in the night; and we heard their groans as they lay by our fire close to us. In the morning they were removed into the house which Sir George Cathcart had so kindly resigned to them. Nothing could have been finer than the weather during the whole march, for we had no heavy rain since the first night we landed in the Crimea; the rain of that night, however, was sufficient to show us what we should have suffered had there been a continuation of it. Strange to say, I did not catch the slightest cold by sleeping out at night, nor do I recollect anyone else doing so.

At eight a.m. the following morning, the First Brigade of the Fourth Division stood to arms, and shortly afterwards a large body of Russian infantry were seen to come out of the southwest corner of Sebastopol, and advancing some little distance towards us, halt, and make a demonstration. We fully expected that they would have paid us a much nearer visit, and drew up some little distance in front on the slope of the ridge, where they could plainly see that we were prepared for them. They however declined the honour, and retired within their walls.

It did not appear that they had done much during the night to their batteries, although they were still actively employed about them.

On the 26th the Cavalry took a Mr. Upton, an Englishman by birth, and a son of Colonel Upton, who built so many of the batteries in Sebastopol. It was said that he remained at home on his farm on purpose to be taken, but he declined giving any information, having once been in the Russian service, and long a resident in that country. We rather hoped to obtain some useful intelligence from him. I am sorry to say that they allowed him to remain at Balaklava; for I have a suspicion that he acted against us. He was permitted to have a good deal of liberty; and from circumstances which occurred afterwards, there is little doubt but that there were spies in Balaklava who were well conversant with the English language. I never could understand why Mr. Upton was not sent to Constantinople with the other prisoners.

On the 28th a cavalry officer brought in another prisoner, who, he said, had been caught quietly walking out of Sebastopol. He stated that he was a Greek, and was going to his wife and family at Balaklava. His very nation caused suspicion in our minds, and he was detained as a prisoner; for we could not allow communications to be carried on between the two places.

The quarry where we were now stationed was full of large stones, which had been cut out in squares, and were piled one on the other. The chips of these stones had been thrown up in heaps with the rubbish, an interval having: been left between each heap, through which the carts had entered the quarry. From their regularity there is little doubt that this commanding position would soon have been held by a heavy battery, formed in this very spot, which was so. situated that it would have swept the country for two miles round. I am glad that they either did not know the value of the position or had not time to throw up works.

Sebastopol, before the war, contained between 70,000 and 80,000 inhabitants, including seamen and soldiers, as well as the artisans in the dockyard. As far as we could see, the south side of the town appeared to be principally built of wood, which gave us great hopes of being able to destroy the place by fire. Immediately after Alma, the Russians sank five line-of-battle-ships and two frigates across the mouth of the harbour, in eight or ten fathoms water, to block up the entrance; and so astonished were they at the defeat at Alma, that these ships were sunk with all their guns and stores on board, ready for service. Their rigging being left standing, their top-masts were visible. By sinking half their ships and closing the entrance of the harbour, the Russians showed that a naval engagement was out of the question, and that our ships would be obliged to try their strength against stone walls.

It certainly seemed very unseamanlike of the Imperial Minister of Marine, Prince Menschikoff, to make such use of his fleet, and to doom it to such inglorious destruction. It may have been a stroke of good policy, but at all events it admitted the inferiority of the Russian navy to that of the Allies.

The south-west promontory which now lay before us is very rocky, and is intersected by deep bays and ravines, which are so winding and deceptive, that many of them are unobserved from this spot; and it is not until the position is changed some little distance to the right or left, that others appear in view. Small parties of Cossacks were seen at intervals stealing quietly up towards us, but they were soon observed by our cavalry patrols, and were compelled to return to their picket at a tremendous pace; it was very amusing to watch them with our glasses.

In the course of the day an orderly dragoon came up to headquarters at full gallop, and reported that about 20,000 Russians were coming down on us in the rear. We now expected to be completely demolished, for we thought of course that another force would come out of the town and attack us in front. Our general moved us back a short distance to protect our commissariat-carts, and after remaining in this hollow, in great anxiety, for some time, it was discovered to be a false alarm; that the force was not nearly so great as was reported, and that they were not coming in our direction. The ruggedness of the land would have been favourable to the enemy, and we naturally supposed that they would have availed themselves of such strong positions. If they had occupied the many defences which nature had constructed for them, it would have been very difficult for our army to advance; but hitherto their total lack of enterprise had been as useful to us, as it was disgraceful to them.

When our alarm was over, we were moved some little distance nearer Sebastopol, where we were to bivouac for the night. Here was a little forest of brushwood. K—— and I set to work and made ourselves a little low arbour, into which we crept; and owing to the number of leaves on the boughs, we succeeded in keeping out the dew. The Russians sent several shots among the Rifles, who had a picket advanced towards Sebastopol; they also exchanged shots with our steamers, which generally saluted them as they passed the batteries; and we could plainly see the enemy's shot falling and splashing up the water around them.

That night (29th September) I went on outlying picket, as each regiment had one, and threw out a line of sentries to protect its own front. At midnight a great beating of drums and sounding of bugles was heard, together with a great clamour in the town, which I reported; but as nothing further occurred, I conclude that they were only sending out reliefs to their working-parties on the mud batteries. At dusk in the morning, two Cossacks appeared for a moment against the horizon on the hill close to us, and I crept over for a musket to have a crack at them, but they turned back the moment they saw the picket. It was just as well that I did not fire, as it would only have disturbed the men in camp. The picket of the Rifles fired a few shots in the night at some citizens trying to escape; and they took a Russian soldier prisoner, who knelt down before them when challenged.

On the 30th, several nine-inch shells were thrown up at no great distance from our camp, by a ship which was careened over in the harbour to give her guns elevation: from the great range they had got, we imagined that they had one of the heavy guns from the *Tiger*. A shell which fell into our camp was marked with the English broad-arrow, and had the English brass-covered fuse. As it did not burst, it underwent a thorough inspection. We longed for one or two guns to answer them, for it was provoking to be fired at all day. A couple of Lancaster guns would have given us great amusement, as well as have annoyed the enemy at their works, with which they were allowed to proceed entirely unmolested.

Sir George Cathcart wished to go in and take the batteries the second day after our arrival, with our division, but Lord Raglan refused, and said that he would not sacrifice a single life more than was absolutely necessary, and that if his present plan did not succeed, he had another by which he trusted to be able to take the place. There is little doubt but that we might have taken it by assault, as Sir George wished to do at once, but it is not likely that we could long have held the position, or that many of us would have lived to come out again. Our amateur friend B—— went down to Balaklava, and was kind enough to bring us up some brandy and a splendid ham, slices of which were soon cut off and placed on the fire. Our frying-pan was a piece of an old broken boiler, which had been picked up near the camp. K—— always did the cooking, and was such a capital hand at it, that I seldom interfered, except to remonstrate with him on his extravagant use of our scanty supply of provisions. This day the siege-guns were landed and parked near Balaklava.

CHAPTER 8

Under Fire

The 1st of October being Sunday, prayers were read, and an excellent sermon was preached by our chaplain, under a broiling sun. The heat was so intense, that men fell down and fainted. Shot and shell fell round us all day, but, strange to say, not one was fired during service. We were not disturbed in the least, though almost immediately afterwards a 56-pound shot fell close to us, and we found that we were quite within range of the guns of the *Twelve Apostles*. It was therefore deemed advisable that we should move our camp out of range, and the following morning we received the order to march. K—— walked down to Balaklava with the letters for England, and I was busily employed in binding together the boughs of which our hut was composed, and slinging them on the pony's back, as there was no wood where we were going. The enemy's projectiles were coming a great deal too thick and near to be pleasant, and we were glad to move out of their reach. It was very fortunate that we got away when we did, for the Russians, having advanced a gun, were busily employed, ten minutes after we left, in throwing their shells into the very spot; and had we remained longer, our regiment must have suffered great loss. A piece of shell had gone through both sides of the colonel's tent, which was the only one there; and another shell burst in a hut which one of the officers had just vacated.

We now marched half a mile to the right, and took up our final position. Here I employed myself in making a hut with the brushwood which I had brought up from the other camp, and had just finished it when K—— returned from Balaklava.

He had found it a longer walk than he had anticipated, it being six miles, and night having clouded in, had great difficulty in finding out our new abode. Our men had been just as active as myself, and had run up a regular forest of green huts on the plain.

From the period of our landing to this time we had suffered as much by cholera as we did at Alma, where our loss was 380 men killed and 2000 *hors de combat*. Our regiment was now encamped behind a hill, and the Russians could not possibly see from Sebastopol more than two or three regiments of the division. On the hill in front had apparently been some old castle or battery, as the foundation-stones were still protruding out of the ground, clearly showing the position of the walls and other buildings around it. It was said to have been built in the time of Catherine II. This became a usual lounge for the officers when not on duty, which indeed was very seldom. Sitting on the stones we had a full view of Sebastopol and all the works, and many a long yarn was there spun as to how and when the place was to be taken.

Our field-battery guns were now unlimbered and placed inside their old foundations. On the 3rd of October, the French succeeded in preventing the Russians from throwing a body of troops into the town, but they afterwards entered on the north side. Our artillery had their tents, which accounted for their being so healthy, whereas the regiments of the line had not yet received any.

The enemy had now obtained a range of 4500 yards, which gave the Light Division, which had just come up, a great deal of trouble, shot and shell being thrown into their camp, causing them to make frequent changes of position. It is not likely that they improved their guns by this practice, but they had an immense reserve of artillery and ammunition, and could well afford an extravagant use of it. I heard that the *Arrow* gunboat steamed past the batteries the other day and fired a shot into the town, at 4000 yards, from her Lancaster gun; and it was said to have knocked down a tower.

When on the hill in front of our camp, the town was quite visible below us, and most of the batteries. On the opposite side was Fort Constantine, a large circular work, with three tiers of guns, and further up the harbour was another large fortification, called the Star Fort. There was a round tower, built of white stone, on a hill to the south-east of the town; and below this were two other forts. On our side also there was a very large fortification, having curtains running inland, a semicircular bastion, and some earthworks, the progress of which now became very visible. We were all surprised that they did not change the colour of the white tower, as it was such a mark for our artillery; but this was soon done by the enemy, who in the course of a night painted it differently, so that it was difficult to distinguish it from the ground about it.

They also moored a two-decker, painted to resemble a three-decker, in the harbour, broadside on us, and springs on her cable. A frigate was inside the two-decker, which amused herself by firing shot and shell at Lord Raglan and his staff, who were making a reconnaissance. The deserters who came over to us gave very little information, but they stated that water was very scarce in the town, the price of a barrel of it being three silver roubles. Doubtless they found it more so when we cut off the aqueducts which supplied the town. This loss must indeed have been severely felt, as they could get but little water from other sources.

It was now decided that the English were to have the right attack, and the French the left; they therefore took up their position in that quarter, and again were close to the sea, as on the march. We were highly gratified to hear that we were to get a thousand sailors from the fleet and a thousand marines, who were to occupy the heights above Balaklava.

On the 2nd of October, Lord Raglan and Sir John Burgoyne made a reconnaissance, the enemy firing constantly at them, but without effect. A very large body of Russians left the town this day, and a report reached us that a force was being concentrated on our right. Some said that General Liprandi's division had joined Menschikoff's routed battalions; and others that Osten Sacken had arrived; but we did not anticipate another meeting in the open field so soon after Alma, for we knew that they could hardly yet have recovered. It was cheering to hear our jolly tars hauling up the heavy guns to camp, singing every tune under the sun. You could hear them a mile off, and if any of us approached them, they would pat the monster guns they were drawing, and say, "This is the boy that will do for them, Sir;" "We're going in 'long with you, Sir," I never saw men in such high spirits as these noble fellows, who had volunteered for this service.

The artillery were also engaged in taking up powder and guns to the windmill, which had been converted into a magazine, and the artillery park was formed close to it. Our engineers were also busy in "stepping" and laying down distances. One party did, as it was termed, "a little foraging," for they came across some goats, which they drove into camp, and I drank a cup of the milk of one of them, the only drop I tasted during the campaign. I also afterwards ate some excellent cold kid, which Lieutenant M——, R.E., gave me one day in the trenches. He can well testify to my having enjoyed it.

Marshal St. Arnaud left Balaklava for France on Friday, the 29th of September, and great fears were entertained that he would never reach his destination alive. He had been suffering much ever since he left Varna, and the day after the battle of Alma was so much worse, that he was compelled to resign his command to General Canrobert; and certainly he could not have given it into better hands. The French landed their siege train in Arrow Bay and Kamish Bay, both places being close to Cape Chersonese, and consequently they had not half the distance, nor the difficulties to encounter, which the English had.

The *Trent, Simla,* and *Jason* brought up reinforcements of heavy cavalry from Varna, about one thousand horses. It is much to be regretted that we had not got them at Alma, for they would have been of the greatest use to us.

On the 4th the enemy had two earth-works nearly finished, and were getting stronger every hour, and they worked away unmolested, with indefatigable exertions. We now received twenty-three tents for the use of the regiment, which were most welcome; for the dews at night were very unhealthy for the men, who were suffering greatly from cholera. The guns which the enemy had advanced were becoming very troublesome: they sent a shell into the camp of the 63rd Regiment, which falling in a tent, exploded, killing a sergeant and a private, and wounding two others. This was, I believe, the first blood that had been shed on our side, before Sebastopol.

This day I rode our pony for the first time, over to the Light Division, to see my old friends of the 23rd Regiment, but found, I grieve to say, but few of them, so many having fallen at Alma; I missed sadly many old faces which had been so familiar to me; and those who had been spared were much affected as they talked over the details of that bloody battle, and the loss of so many of their brother officers. All the camp seemed anxious for work; everybody longed for the batteries to be completed; but as yet we had not a gun to answer the Russians, and it was understood that Lord Raglan was opposed to a desultory fire, wishing to open fire all at once.

A division of sixteen thousand men, under General Luders, managed to get into the town; and a Polish officer, who had deserted, came into our camp and gave us most important information about the number and disposition of the troops, together with the situation of the works and fortifications on the southwest or French side of the town; but he could not tell us much about our attack to the south-east. It was very certain, from what he said, that the enemy fully believed that we should take the place, but that they intended to stand to the last. He further stated that the Poles were only waiting for a convenient opportunity to mutiny and desert to us, but that their movements were closely watched by the authorities.

We were glad to hear of the safe return of Dr. Thomson, of

the 44th Regiment, and his servant, who were left at Alma to attend the wounded Russians. Many of them had died, and others had been sent in the *Avon* to Odessa, with a flag of trace. They reported that they had buried fifty in one day, and that they had a narrow escape of being taken by some Cossacks before they left. A splendid shot was made today by one of our riflemen in the advanced posts, who killed a Cossack at nine hundred yards, to the astonishment of his companions.

It did not appear that the inhabitants of Sebastopol were much alarmed at the presence of the Allies before their city, for we constantly heard of balls and parties on board the ships, as well as on shore. We nightly expected that the fleet would bombard the town. It might not however have effected much good, as the Russians could elevate their guns to such an extent, that whilst their projectiles were falling round them, our ships' shell could not reach the shore within five hundred yards.

I dined with Major D—— and two other officers of the 63rd Regiment, and had a capital dinner of potted veal, fried ham, and bitter ale, as my friends had been successful in getting these luxuries from Balaklava: an agreeable change from the cold "grunter" which I was in the habit of eating. In the evening B—— and I walked over to hear the band of the *Chasseurs de Vincennes* play at Canrobert's tent. During our stay there, the general himself galloped up on his long-tailed grey charger, which was immediately picketed in front of his tent; the band struck up some national air in honour of his approach, a compliment which he duly acknowledged.

The next day (5th) the sailors were busy in dragging up their guns with their wonted alacrity, and great quantities of ammunition were sent up to the artillery park, but it was said that we had not a superabundance of it. Lord Raglan changed his headquarters from Balaklava to a house about two miles from our camp. It was with deep and universal regret that the death of Dr. Thomson, of the 44th Regiment, was now announced: he had died, during the day, of cholera.

Several 84-pound shot fell near the camp of the Second Division, but no harm was done, as it was now pretty well out of range. At 4.30 p.m. we heard volleys of musketry, and found that the pickets of the Light Division had killed several Cossacks. Everybody seemed especially delighted when they heard that any of these rascals had been knocked over.

We were now very fairly off for forage, as there were about a hundred hay-ricks near Balaklava, which the enemy had neglected to burn; but we were obliged to divide them with the French, who had not nearly so great a number of horses.

The cavalry had no very important duties, though they had fatiguing work, and at this time met with great losses at sea. One hundred horses of the Royal Dragoons, and seventy-eight of the Inniskillen Dragoons were shipped at Varna, on board the *Wilson Kennedy* transport and *War Cloud,* for Balaklava. They encountered a violent gale of wind, which, lasting for two days, caused the ships to labour heavily; the horse-boxes giving way, the horses became loose on the decks. It appeared that the captains of these ships could do nothing for the poor animals; consequently, one hundred horses on board the *Wilson Kennedy*, and seventy out of seventy-eight on board the *War Cloud,* perished. This was a sad disaster, and diminution of our reinforcements. The sappers, when tracing the lines this day, were very close to the Russians, I believe within half a mile, but they did not molest or interrupt them in their labours.

On the 6th of October I went over to see the Lancaster guns at the windmills. They looked very much the same as the other 32-pounders near them, except that the bore at the muzzle was not round, but of an oval shape. Great expectations had been formed in the camp and at home as to the enormous range and accuracy of these guns, but the trial of those in the gunboats did not appear to have been very satisfactory; and though there is little doubt that they will be eventually brought to great perfection, it was the opinion of many who had a thorough knowledge of gunnery, that they would not for some time be very serviceable to us.

Everyone was surprised at the long range of the enemy's guns and the accuracy of their fire. The Russians certainly have not neglected the art of war during peace, however backward they may be in other sciences. It is probable however that this war may have been anticipated by the Czar much longer than is generally imagined; at all events, much preparation seems to have been made for it.

Today a council of war was held, and we heard that a gun was to be in position by night,—tidings agreeable to us, as we were anxious to answer the Russian advanced guns, which were so impertinent and harassing, though they did but little real damage. At night we sent out a strong working party of about 2000 men, who did a good deal of work, and fortunately without the slightest annoyance from the enemy.

Chapter 9

Before Sebastopol

The Russian batteries at this time appeared in a very advanced state, consisting of three separate fortifications. On our right was a round tower, containing guns, supported at its base by extensive earthworks, in front of which were a long ditch and trench, forming a very formidable-looking fortification. Directly in the centre of our position was the Redan, a work of great strength, situated in a most commanding position, being between us and a suburb containing the arsenal of the Russian artillery, the marine barracks, the dockyard, and the principal naval establishment of the port. This part of Sebastopol, to which the attention of the British was principally directed, was separated from the town (which the French were to attack) by a deep inlet running due north and south at right angles with the main harbour, into which it falls. A ravine extending from this arm of the harbour, divided the position and operations of our army from those of our allies. Sebastopol, lying to the west of this inner harbour, was defended from the attack of the French by another strong earthwork, called the Flagstaff battery from its having a telegraph pole on it, which communicated with the Round Tower battery; this Flagstaff battery also gave us the benefit of one of its broadsides.

On the 7th (Sunday) we received news of the death of Marshal St. Arnaud at Beicos Bay, and we all deeply regretted that he was not spared to return to France, to reap the honour of that victory in which he had shared on the heights of Alma.

We had prayers and a sermon in the afternoon, and I walked up with K—— to the post-house on the top of the hill, about two miles from Sebastopol, the roof of which had been torn off for rafters for the platforms of our guns. There was a strong picket here, and we had a chat with the officer, who informed us that the Russians had been shelling them all day; and that whenever any parsons showed their heads at the courtyard wall, they were always fired at. Of course we immediately tried the experiment, and a shell was instantly fired, which striking just outside, dapped over our heads, bursting in the road beyond. It was far too close to be comfortable, and our curiosity being more than satisfied, we beat a speedy retreat, thankful for our lucky escape.

After all, there was much bravado in a cannonade of this kind, at this long range of 3000 or 4000 yards. It served only to waste ammunition, and to show us the line of fire of the Russian batteries, for no advantage could be gained by it.

It would be impossible to relate the number of reports in circulation in the camp day after day; but they arrived at such a pitch at last that no one ever believed anything we heard. Guns were reported to be in position, which were to open fire the following morning, but when the morning arrived we were invariably disappointed. The fleet was said to be going to bombard the town night after night, yet nothing occurred at the time we expected it.

On the 10th our tents arrived at a most opportune time, and Captain S——, 20th, K——, 20th, and I took possession of one. It was a bitter cold day, and the wind was from the north, whistling with a chilly blast; and glad enough were we to get under canvas, and the tents were thoroughly appreciated. There was nothing to separate us from the bare ground, which was hard and cold enough; but we rolled ourselves in a blanket, and in the morning found that we were but little rested, having fearful back-aches and sore hips.

There was a little creature which paid us nightly visits, in the shape of a species of mole, or as my servant called it, a "ground lion." He was an extraordinary little fellow, and whenever we dared to take our boots off at night, we generally found them filled with earth in the morning. I laid wait for him one day, and struck at him, but he made his escape: there were numbers of them about the camp. Small green lizards, about three inches long, were also in great abundance: they are harmless, beautiful little creatures, and flit about from stone to stone, under which they vanish at the approach of danger. The centipedes were the only insects we at all feared: they are about three or four inches in length and of a yellowish colour. We found many in our tent, but I never had the misfortune to get one in my boot, where they were generally very fond of concealing themselves. From what I saw of it, I should imagine the Crimea a good shooting country: there were many hares, and woodcock, snipe, quail, and plover were frequently to be seen flying over the camp; and I believe some few officers who had guns and spare time generally managed to pick up a few birds. I heard also of a wolf being shot in the neighbourhood of Balaklava. On moonlight nights, when on picket, the plovers were heard crying around us, and not unfrequently wild-geese flew over our heads.

One Lancaster gun was placed in position this day, and we furnished large working parties for the trenches, which were now being speedily constructed. S——, K——, and I went out on picket at four a.m. the following morning, some distance in front of our camp, and the enemy kept up a heavy fire until ten o'clock a.m. They however did but little harm, considering the number of shot and shell which fell around us; only one man of the 57th was killed, and another wounded. We were stationed at some little distance in rear of the trenches, in a valley; and our men having piled up large stones, built walls to protect them from the pieces of shell and spent shot which were falling at intervals around us. A brother officer, Lieutenant R——, who had just been relieved from picket, and was proceeding home with his men, received a contusion in his leg from a piece of stone thrown up by a shell, which knocked him head over heels: he was unable to walk, and was sent on board our ship, which was lying off Balaklava at the time. Mr. Smith, our highly esteemed friend of the *Colombo,* paid us a visit in our solitude, and after a pleasant chat and a little weak rum and water, he proceeded to the Lancaster Battery on the right, to obtain a good view of the besieged city.

At night the enemy kept up a very heavy fire on our works, which was now and then mingled with yells, beating of drums, bugles, and musketry. It was certainly, for a short time, hot work, and the shot and shell came unpleasantly near. I know of nothing more exciting than shot bounding through the bushes at night, being unseen, and it being impossible to tell what course they may take. Shell however are very different, for you may almost always see the fuse burning; and when in the air, and not coming towards you, it is amusing to watch them.

In the midst of all this uproar of cannon and human voices, our horse artillery were heard coming down the road to Sebastopol at a fearful pace, halting at the picket-house, above the Lancaster battery. An officer was seen riding out half a mile in front to ascertain the cause of the disturbance, as the general in camp evidently imagined that the enemy was making a sortie on our works. I suppose they gained their object by disturbing the camp and harassing our troops. When the salvo was over, and the cause discovered, the artillery was withdrawn, at a far different pace from that at which they had come down.

The succeeding morning was bright, and every noise sounded plainly in our ears: we heard the cry of the sentries on the walls of the town, the rattling of cart-wheels in the city, and church clocks striking, together with guns, which were fired all night at our men and the French, with short intervals between each, during which the only sound which broke upon the ear was the cry of the plover, and the pickaxes in the works below us. It was bitterly cold, particularly towards morning, and my teeth chattered in such a manner that I could not stop them. I did everything I possibly could to make myself warm, and kept perpetually visiting my sentries, who at this part of the siege were well on the alert, not being worn out and fatigued, as was afterwards the case. At this time we had so many parties of engineers, etc., in front of the numerous pickets, that it was not unusual for them to be mistaken for the enemy, and fired into. I never heard however that any loss of life resulted from it; and I am happy to say the mistake was never made by one of our men or officers.

Our engineers and artillery led us to expect great things, and we placed implicit faith in their statement that the place would fall in a week. They also spoke most disparagingly of the Russian artillery, which was then supposed to be in an infamous state. We however found out that this was a great mistake; their fire might have been rather wide at first, before getting the range, but when the elevation and distance of some of their shots are taken into consideration, they were wonderfully precise. I think they had their best artillerymen on the earthworks, as the firing to seaward at the passing steamers was certainly far from good.

My picket was relieved at four a.m. on the 12th, and after breakfast I went with K—— to Balaklava, taking our pony and saddle-bags, to get some things from the *Colombo,* then lying off the harbour. We rode by turns, the pedestrian having a stick in one hand and the pony's tail in the other, which greatly accelerated our journey, and thus we cantered along at a great pace. Many ships were in the harbour, but boats were very scarce: after some considerable delay, Lieutenant B——, of the *Brenda,* ordered his boat to put us on board. We had a sumptuous luncheon on board the *Colombo,* and we were very glad to meet Sir R. N——, of the Guards, who was there on a similar errand. After collecting our necessaries, we returned to camp heavily laden with clothes and provisions. K—— was a notoriously good forager, and he laid his hands on anything he saw which he thought useful, and to which he considered himself in any way entitled.

On our arrival in camp I found that I was in orders for a covering party for the protection of the working parties in the trenches, at 3.30 a.m. the following morning. From our ship we had obtained some blankets, which greatly added to the comfort of our night's rest, and we enjoyed them excessively: our pillow however was but an indifferent one, being simply our tent bag, with a few pegs in it and a little straw.

October the 13th, at three a.m., I went for the first time into the trenches, which were then in a very advanced state; but there was great delay, occasioned by the thinness of the soil and quantity of rock which had to be blasted. This had frequently to be done in those parts of the trenches where batteries were to be formed. We were now 1200 yards from Sebastopol.

The French were enabled to break ground three hundred yards nearer than our advanced posts, for they had not such deep ravines and rocky ground to contend with as we had. They also found clay in great abundance, which was very useful to their entrenchments, and greatly facilitated their labours. The enemy were very active this day (13th) in throwing their projectiles into our works; but they only succeeded in killing one man of the Rifles, and breaking the leg of another. The sappers were busily engaged in laying the platforms in our batteries for the ship's guns, and they found it a most difficult matter, on account of the rockiness of the soil. Lord Raglan visited the trenches at night, and walked from one end to the other.

The covering parties were relieved every morning and evening. The reliefs were obliged to take place after dark, as the enemy kept a sharp lookout for them.

On the 14th there was a very heavy fire on our works, and the Light Division had a little skirmishing. We heard that the enemy had prepared a great quantity of flat-bottomed boats to enable them to retreat to the forts of the north side of the harbour if necessary, and that they were greatly in want of water and provisions. Someone took the trouble to count the shots which were fired at our works on the 13th; they amounted to no less than 1568; and Sir George Cathcart told me that he calculated that on an average 1000 were daily expended on us. I was sitting on the hill in front of our camp, looking at the enemy's fire, and trying to lay down the position of our batteries on a small plan which I had, when Sir George kindly marked out their exact position for me on my map.

The enemy gave us the benefit of all their batteries at ten

a.m. on the 16th, but it was astonishing how little damage was done by them. We watched the whole of their fire from the hill above, and certainly it was a beautiful sight to observe the folds of smoke rising in all directions. It was reported that they did not do much good to one of their mud-works, and that a great portion of it had been shaken down. Probably they did it more to try their strength and range, than with any idea of doing much injury to us. Whilst sitting on the hill watching the fire of the enemy's guns with several officers, amongst whom were several generals, a shot was fired at us, which fell plump under one of the field-guns. We all prostrated ourselves, but fortunately it was not a shell.

Things were now drawing to a close, and it was decided that our batteries would be ready to open fire the next morning at daybreak. Our gallant allies had become very impatient, having reported themselves ready a day or two before. Captain S——, K—— and I went into the trenches on the 17th, at four a.m., with a working party, and were busily employed on our arrival in unmasking the guns, by opening the embrasures; and at daylight the guns in the British battery, and in the French, presented their muzzles to the enemy. At 6.30 a.m. our batteries opened a tremendous fire, which was as sharply responded to by the Russians. It was now three weeks since we had been before Sebastopol, and it is impossible to say how relieved we were to be able to answer their fire. Our guns were loaded and fired as fast as it was possible to do it. The fire from the enemy was beyond all conception, and their shell and shot were accompanied with canister-shot, which, skimming the parapet, and coming through the embrasures, made a most unpleasant whizzing.

Our men were greatly exposed in passing from one battery to another carrying ammunition. The trenches were filled with soldiers on covering duty, lying down with their arms, and many large stones were also in them, so that there was no possibility of their using them as a covered way. All this was occasioned by the scarcity of soil, and we were compelled to cross and recross, almost entirely unprotected, in front of the heaviest of the enemy's fire, on the inner bank of the trench. This was by no means a pleasant service, and many of our soldiers were killed. On one occasion I recollect running down, when a round shot dapped in front of me, striking the ground a yard or so before my feet. It was very odd to watch people running in this way, and stopping for shot to pass them, fancying they were to be avoided by so doing.

Shortly after the fire commenced, that of our gallant allies was heard playing away in right good earnest, and a tremendous roll of cannon, like a perpetual peal of thunder, burst on our ears from our noble fleet. It was, however, impossible to discern anything, from the dense smoke which floated over the town. So constant was the fire, and so good the practice, that it was a matter of some danger to look over the parapet. Great reliance was placed in our wooden walls, and the greatest enthusiasm was heard when they first opened their tremendous broadside. We were almost smothered by the dust and sand which was flying on all sides and the earth seemed to tremble. The activity displayed by our artillerymen and sailors was most wonderful, their guns being loaded and fired as fast as it was possible to do so. An awful explosion shortly afterwards ensued, and our parapets were crowned with men waving their hands and caps and giving hearty cheers. It was reported that a Russian magazine on the left had been blown up; but it turned out, after all our enthusiasm, to have belonged to the French, which was a very mortifying disappointment to us. After this sad catastrophe their batteries were almost silenced, having received great damage from the Flagstaff work which was opposed to them.

Just at this moment poor Dr. O'Leary, of the 68th, who was sitting on the outer end of a traverse with another officer and man, where there was a cross fire, was completely blown away by a shot, and it was some little time before his body was found. The man had his legs cut off, but the other officer fortunately escaped. I had been speaking to poor O'Leary ten minutes before. At this time the trenches presented a scene of horror and confusion. Here and there amputations were going on, and the groans of the sufferers were frightful.

K—— was busily engaged in filling shells for use, and seemed quite an adept at his new occupation. Our sailors and artillerymen served their guns so fast, that at eight a.m. we had hardly any ammunition remaining, and the batteries were nearly silent. This was truly disheartening, and the Russians were firing away almost as hard as ever. Our guns were only fired at intervals, about one shot every ten minutes. The fact, I believe, was that the magazines were not large enough for the undertaking, and it was almost an impossibility to bring down ammunition from the camp under the enemy's fire, which swept the road.

The enemy's works received but little damage, except the Round Tower, which had been silenced by the Lancaster guns at Peel's Battery, and now resembled a honeycomb. One of the Russian magazines had also been blown up. The British batteries were not much impaired, which I think was attributable to their position, as the shot very frequently struck the edge of the hill on which they were situated, and bounded over them, but of course this was not always the case.

The fleet ceased their attack at an early hour, finding it useless to try their strength against stone walls, though I believe Fort Constantine was much damaged. The Russians almost ceased their fire at dusk, and we returned home at seven p.m., not well satisfied with our day's work, and almost smothered by the dust; but we were highly pleased, when it was all over, to hear that the total loss of our regiment was only one killed and four wounded, and one who died afterwards of his wounds, and that there were only fifty casualties in the whole army. Some poor fellows were completely blown to atoms. K—— told me that when one poor sailor was killed, he saw nothing but a blue jacket up in the air, at some distance in rear of the gun which he had been working.

Graves were dug behind the batteries, where they were all buried. I think the canister-shot which the enemy fired did more damage, and was more dreaded than any other, each of them being about the size of a tennis-ball.

The following day, the 18th, I was favoured with twenty-four hours in the trenches, and went on a covering party at four a.m. At the dawn of day the officers in charge of each battery were to be seen anxiously elevating their guns to get the first shot at the enemy's works, so as to be able to judge of the range before the smoke from the Russian batteries should prevent it. The enemy had been most diligent during the night, and had repaired their batteries, so that they were almost as good as new, with the exception of the Round Tower; and the town did not appear in the least damaged. The firing this day was not so severe as on the preceding, as our men had learnt to be more careful of their ammunition, and had discovered that we were not situated like the Russians, who had their great arsenal behind them, to supply them with all that they required. Each gun fired once every ten minutes, but the enemy's fire was greatly improved, and their shot came whistling through the embrasures in the most unpleasant manner.

The full power of the sun's rays came upon us, and there was nothing to protect us from them but a few gabions and fascines, which we piled up in front of us; our men were all lying in the trench, using the embankment as their pillow, when a round shot struck it, and sent almost a ton of soil and sand on the top of them. Some two or three were on their backs fast asleep, with their mouths open: these were completely covered up, and almost smothered.

The sappers were now busily employed in making the magazines larger, and others were laying a platform for a mortar, which was opened that day, but without much effect. It was placed close to us, and we were nearly stunned when it was fired. An order came from Lord Raglan to fire red-hot shot and carcases into the town, and the furnaces were brought down by the artillery under a heavy fire from the Russians, who kept a sharp lookout upon the road which led down from the camp.

The whole brunt of the enemy's fire was now directed on us, as the French batteries were almost silent; and the Flagstaff battery was becoming very troublesome and enfiladed our lines. It is most unpleasant, though very exciting work, to be shot at when in the trenches. We had to lie down constantly whenever the shells fell near us, and it was impossible to judge where they would burst, or the direction of their deadly contents. There was scarcely a shot fired by our batteries or the enemy's during the night of the 18th; but late in the evening it was reported that the Russians were advancing on the Greenhill trenches, and our men were ordered to stand to their arms and the artillery to their guns. It must here be said that the guns were put to bed loaded; and Captain Moorsom told me that he regretted he had not known of the advance of the enemy before, as he would have shoved in a shell the wrong end first, which makes capital grape-shot, bursting as soon as it leaves the muzzle of the gun.

Jack was immediately seen at his gun, cutlass in hand, going through certain evolutions, and showing us how he would cut up "the Rooshins" if they came in his way. I had my glass with me, and could plainly see that the cause of alarm was a few gabions some little distance in front of the batteries. The French opened a few guns on their right attack, but the weight of the Russian metal was soon felt by their small brass guns, and their works were much damaged. The ground on which the French were had been used by the enemy as their practice-ground, so that no doubt they knew the exact distances by landmarks on all parts of it, and therefore could judge of their batteries most accurately.

Just before daylight we were relieved and returned to camp, which was about half a mile distant, and as soon as it became light, the firing commenced as usual from both sides.

The enemy had spent the night in repairing their works. Our riflemen and sharpshooters, who were lying down concealed some distance in front of our batteries, now began again to annoy the Russian gunners whilst loading their guns. They also came suddenly upon some of the enemy's riflemen in a quarry, when the ammunition of our men was exhausted, so they took to pelting them with stones, which the Russians returned in the same way, and it ended in their retiring, after having been severely bruised. The smoke was so thick this day that little could be seen.

Towards ten o'clock the French fire slackened, as the enemy were enfilading a part of their new works. There was an explosion of powder in the Tower battery of the Russians at 3.15 p.m. The Flagstaff Fort seemed a good deal disfigured by the French, but the Redan was blazing away as hard as ever. The sailors were highly delighted with Captain Peel, R.N., who exhibited immense courage, perhaps sometimes bordering upon rashness, though no doubt by so doing he much animated and cheered his men. On one occasion, when a Russian shot had cut away the Union Jack which was planted in his battery, he seized the remnant, and jumping on the parapet, waved it until a new staff was procured. This he did amidst a tremendous volley of shot, from which he fortunately escaped unscathed. On my return to camp on the 19th, I was placed on inlying picket, and at four p.m. was sent again into the trenches in command of a working party.

K—— was also with me, and we were employed in finishing a two-gun battery, containing 68-pound (56 cwt.) ship's guns, on the extreme left of Chapman's battery, to play on the Flagstaff Battery, which enfiladed our works. I had a strong party, and they worked very hard outside the trenches in making the embankment solid, finishing the embrasures, and raising the battery with sand-bags. The sailors who were to work the guns arrived, and complained bitterly of the size of the embrasures; but of course I had only to finish what the Sappers had begun, and it was not for me to alter them.

I here had a long conversation with Lieutenant Greathead, of the *Britannia,* who had the command of the battery. The platforms were laid and the guns mounted whilst we were there. Two other guns of the same calibre were also mounted in Captain Gordon's attack. We were relieved just before one p.m., and in the afternoon of the 20th some sailors from this battery passed through the camp, carrying the body of poor Greathead, who had been killed, together with other men, and they told me that the trunnion of one of the guns had been carried away by a shot, and the gun disabled.

We heard that the ships, on the 17th, had made a large breach in Fort Constantine, and that the enemy had spars from the ships laid against it, apparently to prop it up; gabions were seen on the top of it. I had the whole of the 21st to myself in camp, and felt heartily glad of a little rest. There was a report that 15,000 Russians were in our rear, and our division sent out 1000 men, but nothing occurred, and they returned in the evening. Some deserters came over to us, who being examined by the interpreters declared the town to be in a fearful state; that numbers of killed and wounded were lying about in the streets, and that great sickness prevailed amongst the soldiers. Lieutenant-Colonel Alexander, R.E., died at this time, of apoplexy. He was a most energetic officer, and succeeded Brigadier-General Tylden, who died of cholera just after the battle of Alma. Captain Gordon succeeded to the command of the Royal Engineers.

We were now getting heartily tired of the continual pounding; for it is hard work to batter down earthworks, and the Russians repaired every night the damage we did by day. They had plenty of workmen in the town, but our men were getting thoroughly fagged with being night after night in the trenches. The report from England that Sebastopol had fallen greatly annoyed us, for we felt that a great deal of public enthusiasm would be taken away when that did occur, and at this time that event did not appear at all probable. It was, however, amusing to read the lies which had been so greedily swallowed by John Bull.

A few fires had taken place in the town, caused by our shells and rockets, but little damage was apparent from our position. We heard however afterwards that one fire was most destructive and lamentable, as it burned the hospital, full of sick and wounded, but few of whom could have been saved. Day after day seemed the same to us, and I often sat on the hill in front of our camp watching the fire of our batteries until my head ached. The French were advancing their works every hour, and their fire was beginning to be more vigorous. It was now pretty clear that our batteries were at too great a distance from the enemy's works, but I believe they were placed here for humanity's sake, instead of at 600 yards, as was first contemplated. The Russians had now a new work behind the Redan to protect the arsenal and Government stores, and a work called the Garden Battery, which was very active. They had also got a gun up towards Inkermann, which greatly annoyed our Second Division.

On the night of the 21st a battery was completed, and two 18-pounders mounted on the heights above Inkermann, to silence the guns with which the enemy had annoyed the Second Division.

On the 22nd, at 3.30 a.m., I went out with Captain B———, 20th, K———, and two hundred and fifty men, to a picket-house in the ravine on the left and in advance of Chapman's Battery. It was a very pretty spot, and appeared to have been used as a tea-garden by the inhabitants of Sebastopol, as it is at a convenient distance from the town, and had gardens well laid out. There was also a beautiful spring shaded by fine trees, and a great many caves in the rock, which showed marks of fires having been lighted in them.

The house was well built, with substantial walls, and large, lofty rooms; the ceilings were positively black with flies. Two poor dogs were the only remaining tenants of the house; these the soldiers treated with great kindness. How changed the quiet hamlet must have seemed to them! They must have wondered where the gentle hand that had so often fed them was gone. They still however occupied the door-step undisturbed, and did not seem inclined to follow us. The sappers were busily employed in taking up the floors from the rooms, for platforms of a new two-gun battery which was being made on the left of the ravine above this picket-house, about five hundred and fifty yards from the inner arm of the harbour. This was intended to play upon the shipping below.

From this battery we expected great things, as it was such a good distance for red-hot shot. The picket-house was fall of shattered furniture, sofas, tables, and glass bookcases, which were all broken and cut to pieces. No shot however came near it, which was a comfort, and we sat in one of the rooms and ate our breakfast. The flies here were so numerous that we began to imagine that we were to be visited with one of the plagues of Egypt.

A short distance in advance in the valley was a wall, which, running across, formed a protection for an advanced party, and I was sent hither with thirty men, with orders to defend it to the last. I sent out and posted my sentries some distance in front, at the turn of the ravine, just to the right of the French works; and on the return of my sergeant, he reported to have seen two Russian soldiers sitting under a tree, and to have beckoned to them to come to him, but they sat still and took no notice of his invitation. I ordered my sentries not to fire at single men, as it would only disturb our picket; and as our men were only armed with the old "Brown Bess," and not the Minié rifle, the shot would probably have been in vain. After some little time the report of a rifle was heard, and then another, which was quickly responded to by my sentries; a brisk fire then ensued between the two parties; and finding that we should have a great disadvantage, K—— asked me to allow him to go and drive them in; and my men, hearing what was going on, came up and volunteered for this service almost to a man. I selected fourteen, with a sergeant, and gave orders that they were not to go too far.

The sentries during this time were blazing away, and the French sentries had now crept up, and were beckoning to us not to advance. As soon as our men turned the corner I heard some file firing, and bullets came whizzing over our heads. Shortly after some field-pieces were heard, and our fellows came doubling back, quite blown and in the greatest excitement, each with his little anecdote of what he had done. K—— told me they had driven in the Russians' picket past their picket-house, and had killed three men; but some small battery opening on them, after a great deal of difficulty he managed to make our men retire. One or two of the enemy's picket had remained in the house, and peppered them from the windows as they returned. They did not touch our men, though the grape-shot came very near them.

The sentries were not again annoyed that day, but a poor fellow was brought to the house from the trenches mortally wounded, who died shortly afterwards, and was buried under a tree in the garden. At night the sentries of the 50th Regiment fired into our reliefs, but did no harm.

Lord Dunkellin was taken prisoner this day. It appeared that he was with a working party of his regiment, and getting rather too far towards Sebastopol, saw, by the dawn of morning, a party of men some little distance off. He immediately ordered his men to remain, whilst he proceeded to see who they were, and off he went, much against the wish of some of his men, who declared that they were Russians. Being near-sighted, and drawing too near them, he asked, "Who is in command of this party?" This is all that was then known, for his men, having no arms, decamped on seeing their danger. We had little doubt of his being treated well by them, as his father, Lord Clanricarde, had been our Ambassador at St. Petersburg for some time, and was a particular friend of the Czar. The casualties in the army on the 22nd were three killed and twenty-six wounded.

On the evening of the 23rd large fires were seen in different parts of the town, which remained burning when we went to bed, but it was impossible for us to judge of their extent. Captain Childers, R.A., was killed whilst watching the effect of a ball from a gun which he had just ordered to be fired.

Our armament on the 24th consisted of seventy-one guns in all, not counting ten mortars; the Turks had about eighteen guns guarding the rear. We were glad to hear of the arrival of the *Algiers,* as she had large quantities of ammunition on board.

Our numbers were now being greatly diminished day by day. About seven hundred men had been sent invalided to Scutari during the last ten days, and our numbers did not exceed at this time 7000 rank and file fit for service. Ammunition and forage were very scarce, and our poor bat-horses lived on a little barley, which was now and then issued by the Commissariat.

At the request of the French our fire was directed to the Russian barrack battery, which was giving them much annoyance, and by the evening it was silenced. The Garden battery had also suffered most severely, but they are supposed to have had more than two hundred guns bearing on us and on the French. The numerous prisoners who deserted to us contradicted one another in many points; still they all seemed of the same opinion about the carnage in the town and the stench arising from the numbers of dead in a state of putrefaction. Many bodies were allowed to remain outside their lines where they fell, and were becoming very unpleasant to our pickets.

Opinions with regard to the fall of Sebastopol were very different; many of our officers were sanguine of speedy success, but I think the majority now began to be well aware what a tough job we had in hand, and that there was no chance of the town falling, until one severe action, at least, had been fought, and the place regularly invested. Many regretted more than ever that Sir George Cathcart's advice had not been taken, and the town assaulted immediately after the arrival of our troops. It was, however, impossible, or, at all events, very difficult, to judge at first of the strength of the batteries and the resources opposed to us. Probably, after all, Lord Raglan was right in not acquiescing in our brave general's desire to lead the men to an assault.

I happened one day to hear that a soldier of the 21st Fusiliers had the watch and rings of poor D. R——, which he had taken from him at the battle of Alma. I therefore went to Colonel Ainslie, the commanding officer of that regiment, to recover them for his family, who I knew would be glad to have them; but he told me that he had already made inquiries about them, without obtaining any satisfactory information.

CHAPTER 10

The Line and the Charge

On the 25th of October I returned from duty in the trenches at an early hour, and having taken a short nap, was in the midst of my breakfast, when the assembly sounded on all sides, and the First and Fourth Divisions stood to arms, as a good deal of firing was heard, and volumes of smoke were rising from the valley in our rear. Poor K—— was suffering much from diarrhoea, and was most anxious to go with us, but he was too unwell, and I prevailed on him not to attempt it.

We arrived on the edge of the hill, looking down on the valley of Balaklava, at ten a.m., and discovered that the Russians had attacked some redoubts which were in the valley, had put the Turks to flight who held them, and an exhibition of unrivalled valour had been displayed by the cavalry in a charge in which they had been engaged, and in which they had suffered a melancholy loss. The enemy had attacked the position in the front of Balaklava at an early hour.

A low range of hills running across the valley, at the foot of which is situated the town, was protected by four small redoubts, three of which had guns in them: and on a still higher hill, before the village of Camara, was established a work of rather more importance. These were all occupied by Turkish troops.

It was supposed that the position which the Allies occupied about Balaklava was almost impregnable, the French having also made very formidable entrenchments along the mountain edge, looking down on the valley of a most undulating nature, and our redoubts about two miles and a half from Balaklava. Our marines occupied the hill-sides above the town, more than a thousand feet above the level of the sea; and on the road close to the town was the encampment of the 93rd Highlanders, together with a battery of artillery belonging to the Third Division. The cavalry were about a mile from the town. All this force, together with the Turkish troops, was under the command of Sir Colin Campbell, who had been taken from the First Division with the 93rd Highlanders to fill this office.

The Russians commenced their attack on the redoubt opposite Camara, and after a very slight resistance from the Turks, carried it. The garrison were seen flying to their supports in Redoubt No. 2, some distance in the rear, pursued by the enemy's horse.

At this time the Light Cavalry, under Lord Cardigan, were formed, in rear of which were the Heavy Cavalry, under Brigadier-General Scarlett, acting as a reserve, the whole under the command of Lord Lucan. They were formed close to their encampment, and concealed from the enemy's view by an undulation in the land. In rear of the cavalry brigades, across the entrance to Balaklava, the 93rd Highlanders were drawn up in line. Great reliance had been placed in the Turks who garrisoned the redoubts, previous to this day, as they were said to be so steady behind batteries and fortifications.

When the enemy had taken Redoubt No. 1 they pushed on their cavalry rapidly, and the Turks were seen flying out of No. 2 Redoubt at their approach, rushing off to Balaklava and Redoubt No. 3; great confusion ensued, and the Cossacks mowed them down, with yells, right and left. The enemy's artillery now took possession of Redoubt No. 2, and turned our own guns on No. 3,—and after a few shots had been exchanged, the Turks were seen running off to the town as fast as their legs would carry them.

There were about two hundred and fifty Turks and one English artilleryman in each redoubt. They did not hold the redoubts long enough for the Allies to render them any assistance, and in their retreat they were cut to pieces by the Russian hone. Their troubles ware not over here, for the guard of our men at the entrance to Balaklava received them at the point of the bayonet, and would not allow them to enter, knowing in what a cowardly manner they had behaved.

About fifteen hundred of the Russian cavalry shortly after charged the Highlanders, that "thin red line," who kneeling down when they were within six hundred yards, sent a volley into their columns. This did not check them however; but when within a hundred and fifty yards they were met by another volley, which threw them into confusion, and wheeling about they fled in every direction. The thin British line was quite sufficient for them, and Sir Colin Campbell exclaimed, "I did not consider it worthwhile to form them even four deep!"

But this was not all. The blue jackets of another force of Russian cavalry, with their supports, were now seen advancing towards our cavalry, their line being twice as long as ours, and three or four times as deep, as well as that of the reserve. The Greys and Inniskillens charged these advancing Russians, who were only a short distance from them. The Russian wings then wheeled inwards, threatening our cavalry with utter destruction, but they took a slight turn to the right and went clean through the enemy's cavalry with the most thrilling shouts; and with diminished numbers they charged on to the next column of the enemy. It became now a hand-to-hand fight, and the first line of Russians having recovered itself a little, came wheeling round to take the Greys and Inniskillens in rear: when up came the 1st Royal Dragoons, accompanied by the 4th and 5th Dragoon Guards, who charging through the first line of the Russians, continued their desperate course as far as the second, and with their assistance the Greys put them to an utter rout. The Russian horse, or rather half their numbers, now retired at a fearful pace and in the greatest confusion.

Lord Raglan, who was on the hill above, and saw the whole gallant affair, despatched an *aide-de-camp* immediately to Brigadier-General Scarlett to say, "Well done!"

The brigadier replied with a countenance beaming with delight, "I beg to thank his Lordship."

The greatest enthusiasm now prevailed, and hearts and hands proclaimed their delight, and many a cheer rent the air. The loss of our Heavy Cavalry was but trifling, but they did not pursue their flying enemy very far. Lieutenant-Colonel Griffiths, Major Clarke, and Cornet Pendergast were wounded, but there were not more than half-a-dozen men killed.

At 10.30 a.m. the Fourth Division took up their position in the centre of the plain in front of Balaklava, and the Light Company in front on the left flank, with the Heavy Cavalry in reserve. The guns were on the right, and the 3rd Dragoons and Inniskillens on the right of the brigade, and the Greys and 4th and 5th Dragoon Guards on the left. A body of French cavalry, the *Chasseurs d'Afrique*, also came down to the valley, taking up their position some distance to our left.

The following order was sent to Lord Lucan in the course of the morning:—

> The cavalry to advance and take any opportunity to recover the heights; they will be supported by infantry, which has been ordered to advance on two points.

This not being acted upon, Captain Nolan, 15th Hussars, was despatched with a written order from Brigadier-General Airey, the quarter-master general, to Lord Lucan, containing the following:—

> Lord Raglan wishes the cavalry to advance rapidly to the front, to follow the enemy, and try to prevent the enemy carrying away the guns. Troop of Horse artillery may accompany; French cavalry is on your right.—Immediate. (Signed) Richard Airey.

The order was followed, after a little reluctance, by the charge of the Light Cavalry, led by Lord Cardigan. Lord Lucan saw against what odds they had to contend, and that destruction was before them. The Heavy Cavalry, acting as their reserve, was some distance in rear, together with the Infantry, and it may almost be said that they were without supports.

The Light Cavalry were composed of the following regiments:—4th Light Dragoons, 8th Irish Hussars, 11th Prince Albert's Hussars, 13th Light Dragoons and 17th Lancers, mustering in all six hundred sabres, scarcely making one effective regiment; and this handful of brave fellows went to the front amidst a volley of musketry and a heavy fire from the redoubts. At twelve hundred yards the enemy opened a tremendous broadside on them from thirty guns, which clouded them in smoke, and many fell. Still on they dashed, and flew into the batteries, cutting down the gunners at their post, their sabres flashing above the smoke.

The scene now became very awful: the plain was covered with dead men and horses; loose troopers were galloping about in all directions; and wounded Hussars were riding home to the camp with ghastly countenances, their horses covered with blood. One officer was seen galloping towards the camp, cutting and slashing with his sword, and shouting in a most furious manner: Such was the excitement into which he had worked himself. As the cavalry were retreating, a mass of Russian horse attacked them on their flank: these were charged furiously by the 8th Hussars, who with great loss cut their way through these almost overwhelming numbers.

To the everlasting disgrace of the Russian name, their gunners returned to the redoubts, and turned the guns, with grape and canister shot, on the wounded troopers, who lay in hundreds on the plain which had been the scene of action, and where, they were mingled with numbers of their own men. Such was the barbarian brutality of the creatures we had to contend with! Friend and foe were the same to them.

The retreat of the remnant of our gallant little band of light cavalry was covered by "the Heavies," who had no easy task allotted to them; and though they performed it nobly, they suffered severely in the duty from the fire of the batteries.

The total loss of the Light Brigade was about four hundred

men, and that of the Heavy Brigade, in both actions, thirty-six men. Lord Cardigan was reported to have ridden over a gun-carriage in one of the batteries, and to have received two lance thrusts through his clothes. Lord Lucan was slightly wounded. Captain Nolan was killed by almost the first shot from the enemy in front of the Hussars. Captain Maude, of the Horse Artillery, was wounded at the beginning of the action, and his loss was greatly felt by the army, for he was a very brave and efficient officer.

Amongst the killed were Major Hackett, 4th Light Dragoons; Cornet Hughton, 11th Hussars; Captains Good and Oldham, and Cornet Montgomery, 13th Light Dragoons; Captain Charteris, 92nd Regiment, *aide-de-camp* to Lord Lucan; Captain White and Lieutenant Thomson, 17th Lancers; Captain Lockwood, 8th Hussars, *aide-de-camp* to Lord Cardigan. Captain Morris, commanding the 17th Lancers, received many fearful wounds. He was, I believe, one of the most able swordsmen in the British army, and to this may his wonderful escape be attributed.

Captain Wombwell, of the 17th Lancers, also had a very narrow escape, having been taken prisoner. He was informed by a Russian officer, who spoke French, that their men were rather rough (which he had experienced already), but that they would not hurt him, and that he would be taken care of. Not so however; for in the last charge he succeeded in getting on a horse, and, joining his regiment in their charge, without any arms to defend himself, he reached the camp in safety. Captain Hutton, 4th Light Dragoons; Captain Cook, 11th Hussars; Captain Maxse, *aide-de-camp*; and Lieutenant Trevelyan, 11th Hussars, were also wounded. Lord Fitzgibbon, 8th Hussars, was frightfully wounded, and expired at Balaklava shortly afterwards. During these gallant affairs the Fourth Division artillery were busily engaged in playing on the Russian artillery, and the Fourth Division itself was lying down in line in rear of their guns. This was by no means a pleasant position, and the shot and shell were dropping in great numbers over our heads. Only one, fortunately, took effect on us, wounding a man so seriously in the knee that amputation was necessary, and he shortly afterwards expired. During these affairs two hundred *chasseurs* attacked the battery on the left, and cut down the gunners who were playing on our cavalry, but were compelled to retire with the loss of two officers and twenty-five men.

The enemy, seeing that we intended to cut off their right, retired from No. 1 Redoubt, of which the left wing of the 20th Regiment took possession. Seeing the steady advance of the Allies, they abandoned No. 2 Redoubt, and they blew up and abandoned No. 3 also, but they unfortunately carried off seven out of nine guns of ours from the batteries. One gun was left in the ditch outside No. 1 Redoubt, which was afterwards dragged into the battery again. The Fourth Division Artillery was outside Redoubt No. 1, and we occupied the ditch; and they fired on Redoubt No. 2, which also sent shell over our heads, and a piece of one struck the staff of the Queen's colour which I carried.

Their rifles were also very busy in that redoubt, and the conical bullets whizzed past us whenever we showed our heads. One bullet came so near me on this occasion, that I took the trouble to pick it up and keep it, in token of respect for its not becoming better acquainted with my head. From the position in which we were in the trench, we could plainly see the field of battle lying between us and the Russian cavalry. The infantry had retired amongst the brushwood on the heights, and they occupied the village to the south-east of Balaklava, in front of us.

From our elevated situation I witnessed many heart-rending scenes through my glasses. Poor troopers were standing about all over the plain, wounded; others were to be seen galloping into camp at an earlier part of the day, by twos and threes, in regular order, as if in the ranks. One poor animal came cantering along with his hind-leg broken, and swinging round and round at every stride. Others would be seen with both hind-legs broken, endeavouring to rise from the place where they fell. I shall never forget one scene, so dreadful, and yet one which would have made a splendid study for an artist. It was a wounded Scots Grey, who passed us, his horse led by a companion. All looked so sad: even the poor horse, though not wounded, bowed his head, and appeared to sympathize in his master's sufferings. The poor fellow seemed to be in a dying state, and as he leant on the pommel of his saddle, his pale and agonized face could just be observed under his bear-skin; the horse's shoulder was covered with blood, and yet the poor creature seemed to know with what care he ought to carry his wounded master.

We could plainly see the Cossacks on the field of battle, amongst the dead and wounded, and now and then their gory lance would be thrust through the body of some wretched sufferers, who had in vain lifted up their hands, expecting aid instead of destruction from these savages.

The servant of an officer who was ill at Balaklava, walked up from the field of battle, where he had picked up a Cossack's sword, and shortly afterwards took a poor wounded officer on his back to Balaklava. On the way they were fired at by a wounded Russian. Upon this he deposited his load on the ground, and, walking up to the villain, lopped his head off, and proceeded on his way with his burden.

We watched with the greatest interest a wounded dragoon, who was creeping on his belly from the battle-field, near the Russian horse, to us. Every now and then he would halt and hold up his sword. He was presently spied by the Russian sharpshooters in the redoubt near us, and they opened a sharp fire on the poor fellow. He still persevered, and was shortly seen by a sailor, who had a brass helmet on his head, and was walking about picking up trophies, with a friend, quite heedless of their rifles. They immediately went to his rescue, and carried him on their shoulders some little distance, when he was put on a horse, with great difficulty, and brought into our lines. I do not know when my heart felt more relieved. A brother officer, M———, was busy in shooting wounded horses which were near our redoubt; and Captain B——— and W——— were rendering all the assistance in their power to a wounded Russian officer, by sewing up and washing his wounds, but he died that night, chiefly from the intense cold.

Some swords belonging to the Scots Greys were picked up; one I saw was broken off within six inches of the hilt, and another was complete, only the handle was covered with blood and brains, and a piece of a skull had adhered to it.

Just before dark we were agreeably surprised to hear that we were to evacuate this place and return to our camp before Sebastopol, about eight miles distant, as soon as the clouds of night had sufficiently gathered around us. A strong French division was marched into the valley for our relief.

Thus ended this melancholy day, in which our Light Cavalry had been annihilated; the killed, wounded, and missing amounting to 385, and horses 520, 130 of whom were wounded. We heard that there were several men in camp who had not turned out, being ill or otherwise engaged, amounting to about 200 men. The two guns out of nine which the Russians left of ours were taken from the Turks into our own better keeping. At nine p.m. the Russians fired a tremendous volley of artillery on our works, in honour of the complete victory they were supposed to have gained, and on the arrival of our guns in the town of Sebastopol; but it did us no injury.

CHAPTER 11

Inkermann

At one p.m. on the 26th of October, about 5000 of the enemy attacked the Second Division, with several columns of infantry, supported by artillery. Large bodies of skirmishers covered their advance, but the pickets of the 30th and 49th Regiments resisted them with great firmness. The Second Division, under Sir De Lacy Evans, had the honour of repulsing them with very great loss, which was estimated at 600 men. They took eighty prisoners, and about 140 of their dead were scattered amongst the bushes near their camp. Two officers were taken, one of whom had not long before made Lord Dunkellin prisoner. We had about eighty men killed and wounded. The enemy advanced at first with great firmness and rapidity. Their guns having gained the Mound-hill, rendered them every assistance. We had eighteen guns in position, together with the artillery of the First Division, who commenced excellent practice on the artillery of the enemy, which in the course of half an hour was silenced.

The attention of our guns was now directed to their columns, and a Lancaster being brought to bear on them, did very great execution; and being assisted by our skirmishers, put the enemy to flight in the greatest confusion. They were pursued over the ridges by our men towards the head of the Bay; and it was with the greatest difficulty that Major-General Pennefather could stop them, so eager were they in the pursuit.

The Fourth Division was taken out by Sir George Cathcart, and held in reserve, but our Rifles went to the front, and five

French battalions were pushed forward by General Bosquet towards the position of the Second Division.

Lieutenant Conolly, of the 49th Regiment, on picket, greatly distinguished himself, but he was unfortunately dangerously wounded, together with Captains Atcherley and Bayly, of the 30th Regiment.

The work in the trenches was going on pretty much as usual, and the enemy were now throwing 13-inch shell into our batteries, thereby silencing some of our guns: we were unable to touch the ship that projected them from her mortars. The enemy succeeded in throwing a shell into a French magazine this day, which unfortunately blew up, but only one man was killed. The French began to fortify the heights about Balaklava, it having been resolved to abandon our position in the valley; and their cavalry received a reinforcement of 1000 men.

The *Sanspareil* was moored with her broadside bearing on the road leading into Balaklava, and the sailors had some heavy ships' guns on the heights near the tower which commanded the valley.

Many of the Lancaster guns in the Greenhill Batteries were disabled, some having had their muzzles blown off, or otherwise damaged; but it appeared that these were not originally intended to be on the Lancaster principle, but were old 32-pounders rebored. There was a peculiar ring attending the report and flight of the Lancasters at Peel's Battery, and it was reported by the deserters that they dreaded these guns in the town, having so much greater range and strength than the others. I have no doubt that they will be more useful, and their flight more to be depended upon, when the sailors understand them a little better.

On the evening of the 27th the Russians gave us another salvo, but did little or no harm to our works. They showed in force also in front of the French lines, but were soon repulsed by musketry.

Things went on with the same monotony in the front, and there was but little firing on the 28th, except from our sharpshooters, who now mustered pretty strong, and were busy all day with their Minié rifles, sending their bullets into the embrasures, and now and then picking off the Russian gunners. They were formed of volunteers and the best shots from different regiments.

On the 29th I went on a covering party to the Sebastopol road, which is situated in the ravine which separates our right and left attack. It was about the best place to be posted in during daytime, as it was some little distance from a battery, and few shot came near it. A covered way led from the Greenhill batteries to this road, and latterly the sailors who were relieved from duty went home this way. On either side of the road were huge rocks, in which were many natural caves, which in the daytime were generally filled with our men, who lighted their fires and cooked their rations and coffee there; but at night they were moved down to a wall which ran across the road in continuation of the covered way.

At night a subaltern's party of thirty men or so were sent out some little distance down the road, from which sentries were posted within three hundred yards of the Russian redan, which yawned on us and showed its huge black teeth. This was a wretched station to be on at night, as it was probable that if a sortie was made from the garrison, they would in all probability bring their artillery up this road under cover of the redan, and we should not have been able to bring one gun to bear on them from our batteries. We could plainly hear the paddles of a steamer moving in the harbour, in all probability engaged in mooring a ship in a position to annoy us.

Our men were getting fairly worn out, and it was almost in vain to attempt to keep them awake, though we tried to impress on them the importance of their remaining alert in this advanced position. It was frequently my lot to be here. How many are the men I have sent home from this place seized with cramp! It was so low and damp that it seemed sometimes almost possible to cut the fog with a knife, and the road after rain was like a ploughed field. I generally allowed the men to unfold their blankets and wrap round their legs; but, if it happened to be a moonlight night, this could not be done, as they were white, and would plainly have been seen. How strange it is that they should be this colour, as, together with this great disadvantage, it shows dirt sooner! They soon were in a filthy state, as there was no possibility of washing them. The French blankets are much better, being of a brown colour.

At eleven p.m. in the evening of the 30th of October I was ordered on a working party, with forty men, to the three-gun battery, on the extreme left of the Greenhill trenches, across the ravine above the picket-house, and we were engaged in placing a furnace in position for heating red-hot shot, as a gun was bang brought up (24-pounder), to replace one that had been disabled. It was to throw red-hot shot into a ship which was moored across the inner harbour, and which gave this battery considerable annoyance. The gun had to be brought round in front of the battery by a winding road through the picket-house yard, and behind the battery there was a most precipitous rock, at the foot of which was a valley, through which the gun had to pass.

We could plainly hear persuasive language and whips cracking down below us, and shortly after an artillery officer came to me to make a request that I would allow my men to go down and assist them, as the horses were unable to bring the gun up. We went down, and found eight horses at work. They were fairly worn out, and would not move an inch. We hitched the drag-ropes to the axles of the gun-carriage, and the men endeavoured, with the assistance of the horses, to get it up this little rising ground, but were unable to accomplish it.

It was of the greatest importance that the gun should be in position when the morning dawned, and now it was fast advancing. I requested that the horses should be taken out, and that the men should be allowed to try it by themselves, which was agreed on, and borrowing a few hands from the picket-house, they gave three cheers, and ran it up in no time. The horses were again placed in, and we escorted the gun to its next sticking-place, which was in front of the battery which it was to occupy, and the dawn of morning had now come, and we could plainly see the harbour below and the Russian batteries. This was no place to leave it to be practised on all day, and all praise is due to our fellows for their exertions in moving it from this perilous position into the battery. Great proof of skill and presence of mind was there shown.

The horses had been taken out, and the gun was just being put into position, when all on a sudden it got too much way, the men at the drag-ropes were capsized, and a corporal of Artillery, being in the shafts, showed great presence of mind, by sticking to the shafts, and guiding this heavy piece of ordnance into its position; whereas the slightest hesitation on his part would have precipitated the gun over the cliff, and in all probability have killed a dozen of my men. He received the greatest praise from all around.

It was a great satisfaction to have accomplished this task without any annoyance from the enemy; and at daylight, all being ready, and the fires lighted, we returned to camp.

On the 1st of November I took two ponies and rode to Balaklava, to get my own and K——'s bed and bedding, as well as sundry little stores of provisions from the *Colombo*, of flour, for dough, etc., which made me look like a miller before I got back to camp. It was rather late before I left the town, and I was obliged to gallop my ponies along at a good pace.

I met Colonel Dacres and Captain Hamley, of the Royal Artillery, both of whom I had not seen since I was in Canada, and they stopped me and admired my ponies and the whole "turn-out." After I had left them I soon screwed up a canter, and was going on very comfortably, when my pony put her foot in a hole, and fell completely head over heels, sending me sprawling, and falling on me. Whilst in this position I felt glad that she was not heavy, as her whole body was on me, and it was some little time before I could induce her to get up, and could extricate myself from this unpleasant position. When I got up, I was much relieved to think that no one had been looking or laughing at my ludicrous position, and I resumed my travels. The roads were then hard enough, as my bones could testify, but they were soon changed to an abominable mire. There was nothing to make us suppose they would long remain in a good state, as they were but beaten tracks, and no stones in their composition.

On my return we were delighted to get our beds, and K—— and I set to work and soon had them put together. I never shall forget the luxury of the first night in my bed.

On the 2nd at four a.m. the Russians opened a very heavy fire on our works, and we supposed that they must have discovered the time of our reliefs. Some of the 20th Regiment were going down, and unfortunately two of their number were killed and others wounded. They did not often honour us with this, though they generally blazed away every night at the French for about half an hour.

At five p.m. I went on covering party to the trenches and a bitterly cold night we had of it. Our men were fairly done up, and no power on earth could keep them sufficiently alert. But they were nevertheless confident of success and seemed only to wish that they might be allowed to attack the place and carry it at the point of the bayonet.

We returned at five a.m. on the 3rd, and the whole way home anticipated a salute from the enemy similar to that of the previous morning.

My men were always allowed to straggle on the way home,—the more the better, for if guns were opened on our works, they would stand a better chance to escape; but I always halted them to form, when thoroughly out of range.

On the 3rd of November I was on inlying picket, and on the 4th, working party: it rained incessantly all that night.

Early in the morning of the 5th of November heavy showers fell, and a heavy fog rested in the valleys and on the heights above. Our men on picket were drenched to the skin, and their firelocks were so saturated with wet, that there was little chance of their going off, notwithstanding all our precautions. The church bell tolled its lonely knell at an early hour, in the city, but our attention was not called to it more than on other nights when the same thing happened. In the midst of all this wretchedness I was winding my way, with Captain S—— and a party of men, to the Sebastopol road, on the extreme right of our attack. The trenches on our arrival were full of mud and water, and it was with the greatest difficulty we could grope our wan- along. S—— was more fortunate, and took half the men to the cares. When the morning came we were aroused by musketry on oar right, which gradually increased more and more. We had been posted by the brigadier of the day, General Eyre, who had returned to camp afterwards, but came to us, to discover the cause of alarm. He was accompanied by his *aide-de-camp*, Captain L. G——, with whom I had a short conversation.

S—— was shortly after sent to defend the mortar-battery on his right, where it was anticipated the Russians were working their way. During the night a sharp fellow on a picket of the Light Division reported that he heard the rumble of cart-wheels in the valley below them, which was that of Inkermann; but little notice was taken of his report, as it was supposed that it was merely a train of *arabas* going in or out of Sebastopol, instead of immense bodies of the enemy with their cannon, approaching the very place where this picket was stationed. They were creeping up the rugged heights above the valley of Inkermann, which were entirely undefended, except by a few pickets. Our small army was now fairly worn out, and the pickets no doubt were not so much on the alert as they ought to have been in the face of an enemy. I know it was so, very frequently, when I was on duty; but, despite all my endeavours, I could not prevent it.

Brigadier-General Codrington visited the pickets about five a.m., when all was reported "Well;" and after giving necessary precautions to the officer in charge, and telling him that the enemy might take advantage of the foggy morning, knowing how saturated the arms of the picket must be, he turned his horse's head towards home.

He had not retraced his steps any great distance, when he heard rolls of musketry in his rear, and galloping into camp, he turned out his division with all possible speed. He was right in his supposition, for it was the enemy advancing upon us in immense masses; but this could not be discerned in the early dawn, as it was very dark, and they had their grey coats on.

The advancing lines of infantry poured in a fearful volley of musketry on the pickets of the Second Division, which retiring, contested the ground to the summit of the hill, and blazed away at the Russians as long as their ammunition lasted. The Light Division pickets were also compelled to fall back, and beat a steady retreat towards their main body.

No doubt the object of this sortie was to force our men to abandon our batteries by this flank attack on an undefended position. They evidently expected to compel us to raise the siege, and to drive us entirely out of the Crimea, for their cavalry was drawn up in the valley at Balaklava, to cut off our retreat to that place and utterly to destroy our army.

So confident were they of success, that they erected a telegraph-post on the heights of Inkermann, to announce to the army in Sebastopol, and that in the rear, when we were routed, so as to enable them to make a sortie on all sides, and keep up the panic.

The Russians were greatly cheered and animated by the presence of the Czar's two sons, the Grand Dukes Nicholas Nicholavitch and Michael Nicholavitch.

Their presence, together with spirituous liquors, of which they had partaken freely before they started on this "holy war" and of which they had abundance in their canteens, encouraged them to such a degree that they rushed on like fiends, and fought with redoubled vigour. Indeed, I do not think they would have been induced thus to attack us, had they not been inspired with this "Dutch courage."

The reveille had scarcely sounded in the camp when the alarm was given that the Russians were advancing in force, and the fires which the soldiers were struggling to light in the misty rain were allowed to dwindle down to their former darkness: breakfasts were speedily abandoned, and the firelock taken in hand.

Brigadier-General Pennefather was in command of the Second Division, in the absence of Sir De Lacy Evans, who was ill on board ship. No sooner did the latter gallant officer hear of the attack however, than he disregarded his own health, and buckling on his sword, hastened with all possible despatch, not to command his own division, but to assist Brigadier-General Pennefather by his excellent advice, and carry out the success which crowned their labours, aided by the 30th, 41st, 47th, 49th, 55th, and 95th Regiments. All the troops immediately got under arms, and Sir George Cathcart turned out about 2000 men of his division, the rest being in the trenches. These were composed of the 20th, 21st, 46th, 57th, 63rd, and 68th Regiments, and their advance was directed towards the left of the ground occupied by the Second Division.

The First Brigade, under Brigadier-General Goldie, moved in advance, and the Second Brigade, under Brigadier-General Torrens, acted as its support, until it was discovered that the numbers of the enemy would require the whole force to act without a reserve. The Light Division, under Sir George Brown, also advanced to the attack; it was composed of the 7th, 23rd, 19th, 33rd, 77th, and 88th Regiments.

On the advance of the Second Division, they were immediately met by a tremendous fire from the guns which the enemy had brought on the heights; and there were at least forty pieces which were brought to bear on our advancing columns.

The fog still continued so thick that the troops were fired on by tremendous volleys of musketry before they could discover their grey-coated foes, who were thus rendered less conspicuous. Random shots from the enemy (for they could not possibly have seen our men) were fired with too great effect. The Guards, under the Duke of Cambridge and Brigadier-General Bentinck, came rushing to the front, and occupied the ground on the right of the Second Division.

The Third Division, under Sir Richard England, acted as a reserve, but some of its regiments were called upon before the action was over to engage the enemy.

Thus commenced one of the most bloody struggles ever

known; such determination and fury on the part of an enemy, and such a brave resistance, were never before witnessed.

The enemy were led by vast clouds of skirmishers, supported by dense columns of infantry. Two powerful bodies of infantry attacked the Guards on the right, protected by shot, shell, and grape from their guns, of heavy calibre, on the heights. It required every effort of our gallant troops to resist them; their guns in the field amounted to about ninety. The enemy assaulted a small redoubt, constructed for two guns, but which was unarmed. The Guards displayed the utmost gallantry, until compelled to retire by an overwhelming force; but, supported by a wing of the 20th Regiment, under Colonel Crofton, they advanced and retook this redoubt.

Dreadful, bloody deeds were done, which admit of no description; bayonet was opposed to bayonet, which, we are told, never happened before to the British soldier wielding his favourite weapon. The deeds of daring, and hand-to-hand fights, are too numerous to narrate. Now and then small bands of English soldiers were seen crossing their bayonets with the infuriated enemy, though sometimes compelled to yield to their overpowering numbers.

It was six a.m. before head-quarters were aroused by the roll of musketry and shot from the enemy's ordnance on the heights. Lord Raglan was informed that the enemy were advancing in force. At seven a.m., accompanied by Sir John Burgoyne, Brigadier-General Strangways, R.A., and his staff, he rode towards the scene of action. Volleys of musketry and cannon were then pealing forth, indicating the heat of the action; these were mingled with the cheers of our troops and the enemy alternately. This continued until we really began to entertain fears of the issue of the battle. The shells of the enemy, directed with wonderful precision, spread death over numbers of our men, and the bullets were as thick as hailstones. The tents of the Second Division were torn to ribbons, and many of the wretched horses tethered around were either mutilated or killed. Our small nine-pounder field-pieces were of no use against the heavy ordnance which the enemy had in position. But as soon as this was felt, Colonel Gambier was ordered to bring up two eighteen-pound guns into position, to respond to the enemy's heavy artillery.

Whilst in the execution of this duty, this gallant officer was unfortunately wounded, and Lieutenant-Colonel Dixon was left to complete his task. The precision with which these guns were fired, under the superintendence of that officer, much contributed to decide the fate of the day, and to him are due the thanks of every man there engaged. They had the most marked effect, and were the admiration of the whole army.

By this time our men had suffered great losses, but there had been a still greater slaughter of the enemy. The greatest confusion prevailed, and our generals could not tell where to go, or which way to turn, on account of the fog, which screened the enemy from our view. Their position was only indicated by the rattle of musketry, which poured into our lines with deadly effect.

A large column of Russian infantry was at this time pouring a deadly volley into the Fourth Division, which Sir George Cathcart observed was also out-flanking them; and portions of the different regiments of which his division was composed were maintaining a most unequal struggle against an overwhelming force.

The gallant general observing this, rode down into the ravine in which they were engaged, and rallied them. The enemy had actually gained a hill in rear of the flank of his division; but still his coolness and undaunted courage, for which he was noted, never failed him, and riding at their head, he gallantly cheered them on. My regiment, the 20th, was one that was inspirited anew by his presence. Many of them had fallen, and K—— amongst the rest was here grazed by a round shot, which put him *hors de combat*. He was waving his sword and cheering on the men, when the shot struck the hilt and then grazed his shoulder-blade, which rendered him senseless for some little time; but I am happy to say that, after escaping the enemy's bayonet and the heavy fire going on It was not until two o'clock in the afternoon when the enemy appeared to be giving way, and large masses were then seen crossing the bridge of Inkermann, and ascending the opposite heights, leaving behind them about 6000 dead and wounded; some however they managed to take away.

The enemy lying on the field were about ten to our one, and never was a more fearful spectacle than it now presented. It was calculated that the casualties of the Russians, in killed, wounded, and prisoners, could not have been short of 15,000, 6000 of whom were left on the field.

The British troops actually engaged were about 8200 men, and General Bosquet's Division amounted to 6000: the remainder of the French on the spot were held in reserve. It is difficult to come to any exact conclusion as to the number of the enemy, but it is supposed that they mustered at least 60,000. Fresh columns were repeatedly brought up in front to the attack. The ground was very rugged, and covered with brushwood.

While this attack was going on on the right, the enemy made a sortie on the left, and actually got into two of the French batteries, from which however they were soon driven out with the greatest gallantry, and pursued within their very walls by our allies, who managed to fire a magazine of shells belonging to the enemy.

The only account we received on the right of the trenches was, that the Fourth Division was engaged, and that its gallant general had fallen: but we could gain nothing further that day, until our rations were sent to us the following morning, with orders to remain on duty twenty-four hours more, when the sad truth was revealed.

The total loss of my regiment was—one officer, two sergeants, ten rank and file, killed; eight officers, seventeen sergeants, one drummer, 104 rank and file, wounded; 28 rank and file missing.

We were much disappointed at not being relieved from the trenches, and enabled to see our poor wounded brother officers. We were sitting down in despair when an order came from Brigadier-General Eyre, in command, that the Fourth Division were all to be relieved. This news was most welcome, and we hurried home; but, what did our camp look like? All was disorder, and groans poured forth from the tents, and came piercing on our ears. I went into my tent, and found my friend and messmate K—— in bed, but, as usual, in capital spirits,—and I congratulated him sincerely on his narrow escape, for one inch more and his shoulder-bone must have been smashed. I then continued my visit to the other tents, and found many sufferers, though none appeared in immediate danger: there was indeed great hope that all would recover.

Poor Dowling had however received a mortal wound, and his body was found on the field that day (6th), stripped of all but his flannel shirt: his watch had been taken from him. His wound was through his forehead, and his death must have been instantaneous, which was some comfort to know, as those savage barbarians with whom our brave fellows had to contend were not content to see them on the field wounded, but took advantage of their helplessness to bayonet and mutilate their bodies in the most frightful and barbarous manner.

Several of our men died: they had fewer comforts than the officers, and certainly their case was more pitiable; but they received every attendance and care which it was possible to afford under the circumstances.

The total loss of our armies on the 5th November was—forty-three officers, thirty-two sergeants, four drummers, 380 rank and file, killed; 102 officers, 121 sergeants, seventeen drummers, 1694 rank and file, wounded; one officer, six sergeants, 191 rank and file, missing.

Killed	462
Wounded	1952
Missing	191
Total	2605

I walked up to the 63rd Regiment, after having congratulated my brother officers on their safety, to see whether Major D—— was safe, and found him all right and hard at work in his tent. He had his horse shot under him, and a bullet had gone through the holster in front of his saddle.

I regretted to hear of the death of Lieutenant-Colonel Swiney, and others of his regiment, and that some were in their tents in a very precarious state. It was announced that the funerals were to take place at twelve o'clock.

The body of Sir George Cathcart had been recovered, having received, in addition to the wound in the head (which killed him), three bayonet wounds. We regretted his loss deeply, as he was an officer of the highest merit, and esteemed and respected by all who knew him. At twelve o'clock Colonel Swiney's body, that of Major Townsend, R.A., and some others, were interred in the old battery on the hill above our camp. Lord Raglan and a numerous staff assembled: and the bodies of Sir George Cathcart, Brigadier-General Strangways, R.A., and Brigadier-General Goldie, were interred in separate graves, side by side, the senior officer being in the centre. My own brother officer, Lieutenant Dowling, Captain Blunt, of the 57th Regiment, and others, were also buried around them.

The melancholy duty over, we returned to camp, a hundred yards below, and heard from our officers and men their own anecdotes of escapes and the deeds done that day. The colonel had some slight wounds, and his sword and brass scabbard were crumpled up like paper by a shot: a bullet had actually struck the plate of his belt without hurting him. Colonel C—— had the forefinger of his right-hand much shattered. Captain B—— had a shot through the upper part of his arm; but this did not prevent him from continuing to command his company, the Grenadiers, and bringing them out of action. Major S—— received a bad wound in his back from a wounded Russian, whilst leading his company, but the ruffian who inflicted it had his brains blown out immediately by S——'s right-hand man. Captain W—— received a contusion, which laid him up for some time. Lieutenant B—— was supposed to have received the most serious wound of all in his back, and when he was carried home and lifted out of the stretcher, a ball was found on it. Lieutenant

P—— had his ribs blackened by a ball.

K—— also told me, that when he came to his senses he found himself in a most perilous position, the bullets whistling about him. He therefore managed to crawl behind a small stack of hay; but had scarcely left his former position when a cannon-shot struck the place, and killed another wounded man just beyond him. It was most fortunate that he escaped the Russian bayonets. Soon afterwards he was taken to his brother-in-law's tent in the Light Division, and was able to ride home on his pony. On the 6th Captain G—— and H. D—— rode over to see him, and sat with us in our tent for some time.

We were much shocked to hear of the death of Sir R. N—— of the Grenadier Guards. He belonged to the same county as ourselves. We met him often in the camp, and lunched with us but a few days before the battle. His kind disposition endeared him to all who knew him, and his sad fate will be long and deeply lamented.

The manner in which the enemy's fire was kept up was wonderful; and Brigadier-General Pennefather, who had seen other fierce battles in India, said that he had never heard anything like it before. This gallant officer was also heard to say, "I shall never forget the left wing of the 20th Regiment:" this, coming from such lips, was highly complementary. The wounded were being brought in on litters this day, and large parties were sent to bury the dead. Wounded Russians were also brought in and placed in a yard not far from our camp.

The loss of horses was enormous, and I heard that sixty artillery-horses alone had perished. However, about sixty came galloping into our camp riderless, from the Russian army in the rear, some time before, after an alarm which had been created by some of our guns and the French. Nothing was ever known of the fate of the riders; and this good fortune compensated, in some measure, for our grievous loss. They were fine, sturdy little animals, and were most welcome to us.

Lieutenant Duff, of the 23rd, was taken prisoner on picket, on the morning of the 5th, together with some men. A strange circumstance is connected with his capture. When he saw that all chance of escape was over, he threw his watch into the cave where he was, or placed it under a stone. Sometime afterwards he wrote to a brother officer from Sebastopol, and told him to go to the cave for the chance of finding it there. The officer accordingly went there, and secured the watch for his friend.

The enemy were very expeditious in getting their guns up, and were on us before we knew where they were. A great deal of this was to be attributed to the arms of the men on picket being drenched with rain, and not going off in sufficient numbers to give timely alarm. The enemy, however, were not able to hold their own long; nevertheless they behaved most gallantly.

CHAPTER 12

The Storm

It is impossible to imagine or describe the courage and impetuosity with which the soldiers fought at Inkermann. The whole army was, as I have said before, but small, amounting to little over 8000 men, and it is most wonderful how they were able to repel the large force of infuriated men which had been brought against them. Many of our soldiers had been in the trenches on the previous night, wet through with the rain, which fell in torrents. They also fought without their breakfast, having only just returned from duty, when the assembly sounded through the camps. The worn-out and sickly state of the army must be borne in mind; for the men had been exhausted by perpetual duty in the trenches, with no fuel to cook their provisions with or pots to boil them in. The green brushwood was with difficulty made to ignite, and particularly when the rain was falling on the damp ground. Their mess-tins were but small, and insufficient to boil their rations in, and they had thoughtlessly thrown away their camp-kettles on their march to Sebastopol: so improvident were they for the future.

Being in the reserve, we had an opportunity of observing this state of things. I don't know which were in greater numbers, the camp-kettles or the shakos, but I saw the whole plain strewed with them. It could not have been on account of their weight that they were thrown away, or from their being inconvenient, as they were in brown canvas bags, and could be slung very comfortably behind their knapsacks. When they started, about one man in each squad had them, and they took it by turns to carry them. I do not recollect seeing any bearskins, or Highland plumes, lying about, though the discarded shakos were very plentiful. This is not surprising, as a forage cap is much more useful, and ten times as comfortable. The scene of the attack on the 5th was almost in the very same place where the enemy tried our strength on the 26th of October; but this was most likely a reconnaissance made on the most vulnerable point of our position.

The battle of Inkermann certainly showed, under the most adverse circumstances, the great superiority of our troops over those of our antagonists, and it will probably have taught our adversaries a lesson not easily to be forgotten. The heaps of slain Russians strewed over the valley, presented a spectacle which even the eyes of veteran soldiers had never before witnessed, and this was the best testimony of our great victory.

Prince Menschikoff, in his report to the Emperor, stated that there were present forty-eight battalions of infantry, each of which, though said to amount to 1032 men of the war footing, seldom exceed 600 actually under arms and fit for service. These battalions were commanded by General Dannenberg, who had just arrived with all possible speed from Moldavia, and some of their troops are said to have arrived from Odessa just before.

A great difference of opinion exists as to the numbers actually opposed to us on this memorable day. Some of our generals calculated them at 60,000 men; but even if they were only half that number, it would have been a glorious, and perhaps unprecedented, victory, of which England may well be proud: to Russia, on the contrary, it will be an everlasting disgrace; not because her soldiers were worsted in a fair fight, but because, not content with the common usages of civilized nations, they showed their horrible brutality and barbarism by killing those who had fallen before them, and who in vain implored them for mercy. The dead bodies were also hacked and mangled by these infuriated savages. In some instances, scarcely a feature could be recognized, and they were in such a state that it was often next to an impossibility to move them to the place of interment. Lord Raglan, we were delighted to hear, sent a flag of truce to Menschikoff, to know why such barbarism was countenanced. The Russian general's reply was most unsatisfactory. He denied it as a practice, and made excuse for excitement and anger on account of our having burnt one of their churches. A Russian major was taken while perpetrating an act of horrible brutality. He did not suffer an ignominious death, as was imagined would be the case, but was sent to Scutari, where he was cut and shunned by all his own officers, and died only a short time since, not having any marks of disease about him: probably he pined away, and fell a victim to his own troubled conscience.

Our ambulance-wagons were found insufficient, in the state of the roads after the 5th, to remove the wounded to Balaklava, and the French kindly lent us mules for that purpose, as soon as they had completed their own service.

Information now arrived that we should in all probability be attacked again, and on the evening of the 6th we were moved down towards the windmill; but on our arrival there, it was discovered to be a false alarm, and we returned to the camp.

On the evening of the 7th I was sent for, with a working party, by the quartermaster-general of the Fourth Division, and told that I was to perform a duty that was "short and sharp," namely, to break up and throw a trench across the Sebastopol road, within but a short distance of the enemy's "Redan" Battery. When we had procured the tools, the quartermaster-general accompanied us, together with two officers of engineers, who selected a spot and gave me instructions how to proceed. The moon at intervals shone bright and clear; but fortunately the Russians did not observe us, or open fire from their battery. About twelve o'clock we had a very tolerable embankment thrown up, and had commenced another in rear of the pickets, which, with the assistance of musketry, would have formed a decided impediment to artillery, for some little time. I was often surprised that the Russians never attempted a sortie at this point.

The men were worn out, and it was difficult to get them

to work with any rapidity or energy; but it was naturally to be accounted for, from being over-worked and not having proper food. I have seen men in the trenches by my side, eating raw salt pork and beef like cannibals; and when asked why they did it, their reply was, "We have no time to cook it, Sir." Could we expect anything but disease from the effects of such a diet? The coffee was also a great part of the time in an unroasted state; and how was it possible that this could be used by those who had not time to fry it, even if they had materials for so doing? Up to this time we had received our rations pretty regularly, until the bad weather set in, and the rain rendered the roads almost impassable. The Commissariat used every means in their power; but when the provisions did fall short, it was evident that they had not sufficient stores, if any, in camp, and nothing was to be obtained by them nearer than Balaklava.

Poor Major S—— was anxious to get out of camp, as his wound gave him some trouble, and he procured an *araba* from the commissariat, which was going down empty on the morning of the 8th, and got on board ship safely. Colonel C—— managed to ride down the previous evening, and caught the *Colombo* before she sailed with wounded for Scutari, in which he was very fortunate, as he was sure of every comfort and attention on board our old friend. The others however did not get off until the 9th, when an ambulance came for them. Captain B—— K—— and B—— were sent on board the *Andes,* on which ship, I regret to say, they are stated to have met with but little attention. As there was no attendance, those officers who had fortunately the use of their legs assisted the others as much as possible. It was indeed very lucky for the helpless that people were on board who could render them assistance. I felt very lonely when K—— left; but I consoled myself by thinking that he would return in a fortnight—the time he was expected to be away.

On the death of Brigadier-General Goldie our colonel took command of the brigade, and Captain R—— was again appointed as his *aide-de-camp*. The command of the 20th Regiment fell to Major E——, who had escaped at the battle of Inkermann without a scratch.

The trenches had now become in a most dreadful state of mud and filth, and it was very necessary to be cautious when we sat down in them, as there were many unpleasant little animals, in the shape of lice, to be picked up there, which did not add to our comfort: the tents of the men were also full of them, as well as the occupants themselves.

On the 12th, at five p.m., I went on a covering party to the batteries, with 120 men. I had felt very unwell all day, and had been in bed, and was very unfit to take this duty; however, as we had all to put our shoulders to the wheel, I staggered out. It had been raining very heavily all day, and showers still continued to fall.

On my arrival in the trenches I found a Pole there, who had deserted and come in over the parapet. The soldiers were very kind to him, and he made known to them, by signs, that it was posted about Sebastopol, that the Allies cut off the ears and noses of those who deserted to them. How agreeably surprised he must have been when he found the scissors were not applied to him! Those in charge of him were anxious to hand him over to my tender care, but I thought he would be of much more use at Head-quarters, and would not accept him; accordingly he was taken to the camp, and appeared very happy under existing circumstances.

About midnight we were aroused by the report of rifles, and bullets whizzing over our heads. It appeared that the Russians in "the Ovens" were blazing away at our advanced sentries, and the French on the left. Accordingly we fixed bayonets and stood to arms, and I received orders from the officer in command of the trenches, to be ready to charge them outside the parapet, in the event of the enemy advancing on us. A salvo was fired on the French works, as usual, and volleys of musketry; but nothing further occurred, and we settled down on our haunches again.

It was a bitter cold night, and the wind searched into every corner and crevice of the batteries. I felt very unwell, and reported it to the commanding officer, who kindly said he would dispense with my services, but that if I remained until the morning, he should not require me to be relieved by another officer. Knowing how hard the work was, and how short of hands we were, having only five subalterns for duty, I determined on remaining, and proceeding home at the dawn of day. Heartily glad was I to crawl home when it arrived. I immediately went to bed, and was laid up for some time with rheumatism and fever. The rain fell in torrents that day, and our poor men had great difficulty in cooking their provisions. The whole camp was like a well-trodden ploughed field, nothing but mud and slush.

Our tent was so old and thin, that the rain came through in great quantities; but I fortunately had a waterproof sheet, which I laid over my bed, and it rendered me great service. But the men however had not these luxuries, and had to fight against the elements as best they could. The tents were crowded to excess, and for some time they had as many as twenty men in each, and consequently swarmed with vermin. The men's clothes were torn and in a filthy state, and their boots were in tatters on their feet; they had purchased some French-made boots at Balaklava for seven or eight shillings a pair, and these had come to pieces as soon as the first rain fell. No one can form an idea of the wretched picture the British soldier presented at this period, or of his emaciated appearance.

It blew fresh on the 13th from the south-west, but there were no indications of worse weather, and the night was comparatively fine, and at intervals almost calm. Towards daylight on the 14th however a gale came on, which, at 6.30 a.m., grew into the most fearful hurricane ever remembered in that country. This was accompanied by thunder and lightning and torrents of rain.

Being ill, and not likely to be called out, I had unfortunately undressed myself, and I had not time to put on my clothes before our tent was blown quite over our heads, inside out, the pole at the same time falling on my head, with swords and things which hung around it. The wind was blowing so furiously that the sea of mud which was before us was blown up in our faces, and covered everything about us. I looked in despair at S———, who was in a roar of laughter; while our servants were standing around, unable to move for amazement. All the neighbouring tents had shared, or were sharing, the same unhappy fate.

My eye caught R———'s tent still standing, and I told my servant to carry me in my bedding to it. The poor wretch stopped half-way, and looked in my face, as much as to say, he could carry me no further, and I was in the greatest fear of being precipitated headlong into the mud: however he staggered on, and deposited me in the tent on R———'s bed, which he most kindly prepared for me. I found him holding on, in the most determined manner, to his tent-pole, which was reeling about very suspiciously. Tentless friends came in all the morning, and they were sworn into the service, and by their united exertions it weathered the gale; others were walking about in their cloaks, drenched to their skin, seeking shelter from the pitiless storm. Eyes were cast to the other divisions, and we found they were in the same plight as ourselves; all except the Turks, who seem better to understand the art of tent-pitching.

Our thoughts, however, turned to the fleet, and we became anxious about the poor ships, for we felt that many must have inevitably been wrecked on the inhospitable, iron-bound shore; but from the hill on which we were, nothing could be discerned by some officers who went up to it. Breakfast was out of the question, but later in the morning my servant, in the most thoughtful manner, made me some tea, and we divided it amongst our small party. Although I was ill, I was much better off than the poor fellows in the hospital, as the marquees were all down, and they were in the open air, exposed to the harsh gale.

In the afternoon it was officially reported that seven ships, laden with commissariat stores, had been wrecked outside Balaklava harbour, and the loss of life was reported to be awful. Inside the harbour of Balaklava the ships were grating and smashing one another to pieces, and the water was strewed with boards and planks of every size.

Colonel D——, of the 63rd Regiment, being tentless, came down to see if there was any chance of shelter in mine, but he found it prostrated, and sat with us for some time, talking over our troubles. More formidable enemies than the Czar had taken up arms against us,—winter, the storm, and the hurricane. How our poor fellows were to stand them we could scarcely imagine! Towards evening the storm abated, when the Russians made a sortie on the French, but were vigorously repulsed. The rows in this quarter were of nightly occurrence, and about eight o'clock in the evening we always expected them in some shape or other; but our gallant allies were seldom surprised, and met with no considerable losses.

Scenes of a sad nature had been witnessed outside the harbour of Balaklava. Among the disasters, the wreck of the *Prince* was the most appalling. This splendid steamer was about 2700 tons, and had not long been bought by Government. She was laden with winter-clothing for the troops; consisting of woollen frocks, 53,000; woollen socks, 35,700; watch coats, 2500; flannel drawers, 17,000; rugs, 3700; blankets, 16,000; together with medical stores and other necessaries. The *Prince* was a new ship, and brought the 46th Regiment, which was landed previously to the gale; but through some negligence her cables had not been clinched, consequently she lost two anchors, one after the other, in forty fathoms, outside the harbour. Steaming out to sea she prepared another cable, and letting it go, she held to it until the gale came on, when it snapped, and she drifted on the rocks. The captain cut away her masts, and the rigging got unfortunately entangled in the fans of the screw, which rendered her machinery useless; otherwise she might have got to sea. Out of a crew of about one hundred and fifty, only six or seven were saved.

We felt the loss of this vessel very much, for of course it affected our men, who were in such a pitiable condition. Many of the transports were laden with hay and forage for the horses. This was also very sad, as these poor creatures were in a wretched state, with scarcely a pound of flesh on their ribs; in fact, in such a weak state that it was reported one of them was blown over in the gale, and I have no doubt this was true enough. The total loss of lives at Balaklava was about three hundred and fifty. Amongst the transports which were lost were the *Caduceus,* abandoned; the *Marquese,* all hands lost; the *Wild Wave,* one or two saved; the *Rip van Winkle,* all hands lost; the *Kenilworth,* all hands lost; the *Progress,* some saved; the *Resolute,* all hands lost the *Wanderer,* all hands lost; the *Mary Ann*, all hands lost; the *Pultowa,* all hands saved; besides many others which were dismasted and otherwise damaged, so as to render them unfit for further service.

Many casualties in the transport service also happened at Katcha, as well as amongst the fleet. Transports got adrift, and parting from their cables, fouled one another, as well as the ships of the fleet. The *Samson* was dismasted, and made a total wreck, by two transports getting foul of her, but fortunately was not driven from her anchors. The *Terrible* drifted close inshore, but fortunately, with her paddles, she was able to contend with the elements, and steam out to sea.

The *Retribution,* with the Duke of Cambridge on board, had a very narrow escape, and lost her rudder. She was obliged to throw her upper-deck guns overboard. She was called by the Russians the *Black Cat,* because she was always prowling about. Numbers of our splendid transports, amongst which were the *Pyrenees, Lord Raglan, Rodsley,* and *Ganges,* went ashore here, together with some eight small French brigs. Several lives were lost, and some fell into the hands of the Cossacks, who were ready to pounce on their booty; but the boats of the fleet, in the most gallant manner, rescued an immense number the following morning, when the vehemence of the gale had abated.

Similar disasters had occurred at Eupatoria, where the sea ran with unbroken violence, being a most exposed anchorage. A Turkish line-of-battle ship and the French *Henri IV* were driven on shore, and partly buried in the sand, so that there was no possibility of removing them. The latter ship was converted into a battery, and some artillery were left on board her, to keep the beach clear of Cossacks. Many other ships also shared the same fate. We were all in great anxiety to know where our old friend the *Colombo* was during the tempest, and I am happy to say she was safe at Constantinople. The Turks lost a line-of-battle ship in the Bosphorus, and there was a report that they had only three left in their service. The gale however was not so violent at Constantinople, though some minarets were blown down, and other accidents happened.

S—— managed to get our tent pitched again on the 15th, and I returned to it; but it was so smeared with mud, that it had a most melancholy appearance. Ever afterwards we were in fear and trembling that the first squall we should be left in the same predicament in which we were on the 14th, as there was no holding for the tent-pegs in the sea of mud in which it was pitched.

News came that General Liprandi had broken up his camp at Balaklava, and had retired beyond the Tchernaya. This was welcome intelligence, as we felt that we could not attack Sebastopol with their armies in the rear. The Russians had sunk another ship across the entrance of the harbour, she haying drifted from her moorings to this place during the gale.

The enemies advanced pickets had taken up a position in front of the Greenhill trenches, which worried the troops in the batteries, and gave them great annoyance, at the same time taking in reverse the French works, and giving them equal trouble. On the night of the 20th November Lord Raglan ordered them to be dislodged by a detachment of the 1st battalion Rifle Brigade, under Lieutenant Tryon. A most gallant affair took place, which was most effectually performed, though unhappily attended by the death Of Lieutenant Tryon, nine men having been killed and seventeen wounded. Shortly after the attack this officer saw a man going to the rear, and asking him the reason, he said he was badly wounded in the hand; on which Lieutenant Tryon took his rifle and ammunition, and was engaged in loading it, when he was shot through the head.

Several ruined ovens of a large size were occupied by Russian riflemen, who were enabled to pick off the gunners in the

Greenhill batteries. Our gallant little band drove them out of their stronghold, in such a manner as to call forth, not only an order from the commander-in-chief, but also from General Canrobert to the French army, in which he spoke in high terms of the gallant officer, Tryon, who had fallen, and held him up as a noble example to the troops under his command.

Lieutenant Tryon had long been anxious to be allowed to undertake it. He was an excellent rifle shot, and fired about two hundred rounds at the battle of Inkermann, out of which he said he had no doubt one hundred and fifty took effect. His loss was deeply felt by all who knew him, as well as by the men of his regiment, by whom he was respected and beloved. By his sad death Her Majesty lost a most devoted servant, and an officer of the highest merit.

Chapter 13

I Fall Ill

In a despatch General Canrobert stated that it was his opinion that up to this period (the 22nd of November) the enemy had expended 400,000 shot and 1,200,000 kilograms of powder, since our arrival before the walls of Sebastopol. We heard from deserters that some of their powder was very bad, and unfit for use, being, like their ships, contracted for. The Russians gave the French the benefit of a tremendous fire on the 22nd, but their efforts were attended with no loss to our allies or damage to their works.

The British force now received a reinforcement from the 97th Regiment, who marched up to camp with band playing. I was fortunate to be able to get up my baskets and other articles from the *Colombo*; and my servant and pony arrived at a late hour, tired out from the dreadful state of the roads, for it was a day's work to go to Balaklava and back. I was in a wretched state of weakness, and did not see much chance of my health improving, since for many days I could not get any fresh meat from the hospital, and was obliged to live on biscuit and tea. Whilst in this state R―― received a box from Mr. G――, of the *Vengeance,* in which were a loaf of bread for me and a bottle of wine. The bread was a fortnight old, and rather mouldy, but, barring the crust, it was a great luxury, and lasted me for some time. Every third day my servant was obliged to go away some distance for fuel, and to pick up small roots and chips of wood, as it was almost an impossibility to make fires of the green brushwood which the soldiers used, in rainy weather. This took him some hours, and it generally ended in my losing my dinner altogether, and contenting myself with a cup of tea.

At this period the men only remained in the trenches twelve hours at a time, which was a great relief to them, and I believe this course was first proposed by Lord W———. It was impossible to procure any sort of comfort for them at Balaklava. I lent my pony, and sent my pay-sergeant down frequently, but he was unable to procure any flannels, or woollen comforters, socks, or anything that might be useful. He bought some boots there, which fell to pieces the first time they were used in the mud, and this was a total loss to the poor fellows. The town was full of "sharks," but I think the prices in some instances were made exorbitant by the masters of transports selling things to the shops from their stores at frightful prices. It is to be regretted that some of the shopkeepers and robbers were not turned out of the place, for then we might have been able to obtain provisions, at a price something like their value.

M——— and I sent my pony to Balaklava for some potatoes and onions, if the servant could buy them; and he brought us a sackful, for which he paid nothing, having been allowed to help himself on some steamer, together with a number of soldiers. Difficulties arose at this time in the Commissariat Department. The store of pork and biscuit being exhausted, we were asked to allow our bat ponies to go to head-quarters (about two miles) for biscuit for the Fourth Division, as the roads were in such a state that it was almost impossible even for an *araba* to move in them. Accordingly they were mustered and despatched. How my poor animal existed I can hardly tell, as she had no hay, and only a very little barley, which was issued very irregularly, and we had to send for it ourselves to Balaklava. With all this hard work my poor pony presented me with a foal, and nearly died; but I am happy to say, when I left, a short time afterwards, she was quite as well, or rather better, than could be expected. I was able to leave her with S———.

On the night of the 29th the Russians made a most vigorous sortie on the French advanced battery, which mounted ten guns; and I fancy they anticipated the guns were either disabled or worn out, as they had not been fired for some time: it was a stormy, dark night, with a very high wind and rain, and they attempted to destroy it. It was not much more than 110 yards from the Russian Flagstaff Battery, and had done great damage to it. An unusual noise was heard about midnight by the French picket. One of them immediately crept forward unobserved, and found a strong body of the enemy mustering inside their works. On his giving the alarm 700 French sallied forth to meet them. The enemy, numbering about 3000, sent a volley of balls at them, without effect, when the French sent in a shower of Minié bullets, which caused them to waver, and the French then charging them, they fled in the greatest confusion, leaving behind them an officer and 250 men. The loss of the gallant little French band was nine officers and ninety men, killed and wounded. We could plainly hear the firing at night in our camp, but after listening a little time we used generally to say, "It is only the French!" and turn over and go to sleep again, so frequent were the sorties and skirmishes in their quarter. [1]

At this time I used to lie awake nearly all night, troubled with my cough and rheumatism, sometimes in a burning fever, and at others quite the reverse. No one, however, but those who have been ill in a tent, know the misery of it.

On the 30th of November (St. Andrew's day) the Grand Duke Michael, Prince Menschikoff, and General Liprandi made a grand reconnaissance of the English lines, and every one accordingly expected an attack; but the Russian army was still to the north of the Tchernaya, whither they withdrew after the battle of Inkermann.

It was now decided by the medical men that I, ought to go to Balaklava for a few days to recover my health, and accordingly, on the 3rd, the principal medical officer of our division came to see me, and decided that I was to go thither and remain on

---

1. The French were so near the Russian batteries, that the enemy's sentries used to exasperate them by crying out "Moscow! Moscow!"

board ship for a week or two. Consequently an application was drawn out, which had to be signed by six different people before I could obtain leave to go thither for a fortnight.

The country was a perfect quagmire, and you could scarcely discover the road, except that it was in a little worse state than the ground through which it ran. I waited a day or two for an ambulance, and at last, on the 5th, when tired of waiting, I decided on riding down with my servant, and borrowed Colonel D——'s pony, my own being ill. My servant filled my saddle-bags with a few necessaries, and I managed to get on the animal, and turned his head straight across the mud to Balaklava. D—— had been down often to sit with me in my tent whilst I was ill, and he now came and walked a little distance with me; but I at last prevailed on him to return, as it was almost impassable for a pedestrian.

I felt very ill on the road, but my servant kept close to me, and every now and then I was obliged to make a halt and start afresh. The mud was fearful, and there were numbers of dead horses near the French camp, in every stage of decomposition. I even saw two bullocks, which had fallen down in an *araba*, and not being able to rise from weakness and exhaustion, had been relieved by death. Many of the carcases had been skinned, and the hides used for the roofs of huts; but very few appeared to have been buried. I met six artillery-horses drawing a limber-wagon, that could scarcely move their load, which was a truss of hay. It resembled more a Canada swamp than anything I had ever seen.

On reaching the edge of the plateau looking down on the valley of Balaklava, I could plainly see a large body of Russian cavalry occupying their old position, while the Cossacks were on the hill where formerly our redoubts stood. The worst part of the road now lay between us and

Balaklava, and I met several bat-horses and men plodding their way to camp. One cavalry officer remarked to me that they were fine roads to belong to the quartermaster-general and engineers. Another officer whom I met outside the French lines told me that the assembly had sounded, and that the Russians were advancing. This was not pleasant intelligence for me, as they were only two miles off, and I could not possibly have gone out of a walk, if all the armies of the Czar had been coming down on us. I consoled myself however by seeing the *videttes* circling in the right direction, and from this quarter I did not fear any danger.

After four hours' ride I arrived at Balaklava, the streets of which were crowded as usual, and a regiment of dragoons, which had come down for a short time to be quartered near their forage, with their horses, blocked up the narrow road. The horses looked in a miserable plight. Several bodies of Turks were being carried out to the place of interment, which, by the way, will be likely to breed a pestilence when the hot weather arrives. It is on marshy ground, in a level with and at the head of the harbour; and many graves which were now open were full of water; moreover it is close to the town. I heard of a Turk supposed to be dead having been brought here for interment, when suddenly he rose up and walked home to Balaklava!

I had great difficulty in finding the principal medical officer, who happened to be out at the time. Dr. Lawson however gave me an order to go on board the T—— transport, at that time receiving sick. She was lying close to the wharf, but it was some time before I could get put on board. On producing my certificate to the master, I was shown into a cabin without a vestige of any furniture of any kind, except a looking-glass, which was about the very last thing I then required. No bed or mattress was to be had at any price, so I told my servant to return to camp the following day and bring down my camp-bed. In the meantime I begged the steward to make his way into a bale of Government blankets in the hold, in which I slept that night, and a pretty hard time I had of it. Several invalids had been put on board that day, and one soldier was dead when he arrived on the stretcher! There was only one officer besides myself, Captain C——, 5th Dragoons, who was very ill.

It would be impossible to describe the feeling I experienced the first night when I found I had something more than canvas between me and the firmament of heaven, and that I could bid defiance to the rain which was pattering on the deck. The following day my servant came down with my bed, and I got up for a few minutes to have it put in the berth, but I felt extremely ill after the exertions of the previous day. Our medical officer, Dr. D——, in charge of the ship, came on board and took up his quarters next to me. He had two assistants on board, S—— and W——, but the former was removed to another ship shortly after his arrival.

Nine poor fellows were put on board on the evening of the 6th of December, and had some arrowroot and port-wine given them, and were made comfortable for the night, when notice came that they had gone to the wrong ship. Accordingly they were turned out in the cold, and taken off to another vessel which was loading in the harbour. They had come down from camp that day. The master of the transport came in to see me, and told me that he wanted to get out of the harbour, that it was full of arms, legs, and pieces of flesh, which were floating about in all directions, and that the trunk of a body had washed on his cable that morning. He told me that he had lost some of the officers and men of his ship by fever, and was afraid he should lose more.

The ships were lying very close together, and there was but little room for air to circulate freely. I purchased a box of provisions for my brother-in-law, Colonel D——, of the master of the ship, and I could easily imagine how it was such ruinous prices prevailed in the shops on shore. We heard that some steamer had come out of Sebastopol and had enfiladed the French batteries, causing great damage and loss of life. The fact was, that the Russians had very craftily left a channel where their smaller ships could get in and out, though it was rather intricate. The French had also erected new batteries above the valley of Inkermann. They mounted ten 32-pounders, and commanded the enemy's works and harbour. A French division was encamped near to support it.

The ship was getting her complement of sick very rapidly, and it was said that there was every probability of her sailing in a day or two. Dr. D—— said that I was not improving, and recommended me to be sent to Scutari, a course of which a Medical Board approved. It was also determined that Captain C—— should go. Dr. D—— was making every preparation in his power for the comfort of the poor men on their voyage, and considering that the cases under his care on board, generally speaking, wanted good feeding more than physic, he applied for some sheep. This took a considerable time. First, the master of the ship had to make the requisition; then the doctor had to sign it; after which it was sent to the agent for transports, Captain Christie, for his signature, which valuable document was then presented to the Commissariat, who gave him in return fifteen miserable little creatures, two or three of whom had their throats cut on arrival on board, to prevent their dying a natural death.

On the 12th of December we slipped our warps and went to sea in tow of a small steamer. I happened to be out of bed at the time, and could not help admiring the iron-bound shore which we were now leaving behind us. It was a charming and unusually warm day, and the distant cannon could be plainly heard booming across the water. Sebastopol however could not be seen, as Cape Chersonese shut it out from our view.

We proceeded very steadily on our course; but there was a light breeze, which at night died away, and the ship being without ballast, rolled in a way I had never experienced before: chairs, tables, crockery, being unlashed, rolled from side to side, and the noise was dreadful. We could plainly hear the poor fellows between decks moaning away after every great lurch, and crying out for the orderlies, who, by the bye, were as much like patients as many others on board.

Some of the sufferers had broken legs and jaws, which of course gave them frightful pain as they rolled from side to side on the deck. They had no cots or partitions to lay hold of, and their sufferings must have been intense; over this calamity however we had no control, and they rolled with the ship from side to side, which of course prevented their bones uniting. Several men died daily, and constantly bodies were launched into the deep, over whom Captain M——, 88th Regiment, read prayers. He was on board in charge of the troops.

We had favourable weather, fortunately, after the first night, and sailed on very quietly. It was reported that we were off the Bosphorus on the 15th; but there seemed to be a difference of opinion between the master and mate as to its course, and we sailed up and down, endeavouring to make it on the 16th. The wind was light, and we could not get in that day, but remained tacking about amongst a host of ships bound in the same direction as ourselves.

The 17th was a fine day, and the wind being a point or two more in our favour, we tacked some little way down the Bosphorus, bringing-to just above Beicos Bay, under a hill, where the 20th Regiment had been encamped in the summer. There was a Turkish village close to us, and our boat went ashore for milk and eggs, which were a great luxury, as I had not tasted the latter since I left that place in the beginning of September. The *Colombo,* the ship in which I had spent so many pleasant hours, passed down the Bosphorus, and I was glad to see her, even at that distance.

On the 18th I went on deck for a short time; poor C—— was fast sinking, and his cough denoted that his death was not far distant. I sat with him for some time, and he related to me the history of his life; his mind seemed to wander far from his own sufferings, and by his side lay a packet of letters, which he seemed to value much. His servant was very attentive and kind to him.

That magnificent ship the *Royal Albert* passed us full of troops, on her way to the Crimea. She is, I think, the handsomest ship I ever saw. Her approach was acknowledged by the little forts on the water's edge, which dipped the Crescent as she passed. As the wind still held to its old quarter, the master of our transport went to Constantinople to request Admiral Boxer to send a steamer to tow us to Scutari; but he was told that all hands were so fully employed, that he feared he could not send one; so our skipper returned at a late hour, but rather confident that a steamer would come the following morning.

M—— and D—— however were not so confident, and started for Scutari in a *caique* to see Lord William Paulet, who commanded in the Bosphorus, in order to procure a tug, as our men were dying in great numbers. Next day the *Triton* came up for us, and heartily glad were we to get under weigh. I was too unwell to go on deck, once more to enjoy the sight of the Bosphorus and its beautiful scenery.

We arrived at Scutari in the afternoon of the 20th, after a voyage of eight days, during which we had lost thirty men. Our invalids, as may be imagined, were rejoiced to get there, and expected to go on shore immediately; but the crowded state of the hospital prevented their being landed for some little time. They had however received many medical comforts on the voyage, in the shape of arrowroot, sago, mutton-broth, port-wine, etc., which their kind and attentive doctors ordered for them. One poor fellow died immediately after his dinner, about which he had been quarrelling, and, I suppose, had over-exerted himself. Many of the poor men were in the most filthy state, and the medical men came up from the decks looking wan and ill. The worst of the blankets had however been destroyed, and replaced by others, and additional ones had been issued at D——'s request; in fact, every care and attention was taken of the sick, but the ship was totally unfit for the duty assigned to it.

The galley was not large enough for the cooking of two separate diets at the same time. Invalid ships should be fitted with cribs and partitions on the deck for the worst cases; and the sick should always be conveyed in steamers, or be towed down.

Poor C—— was taken ashore on a stretcher a day or two after our arrival, and was attended by the nurses, and offered anything he might wish for; but he refused everything. Dr. W—— went to see him, and told me that he feared his last hour was coming. The next day his servant came off to the ship, and told us that he was dead. He also said, that he was senseless for some time before he died, and that his hair turned perfectly grey in six hours.

Most thankful was I to a merciful Providence for having spared me from a like sad fate, and for having preserved me through the many perils of war and sickness which I had undergone during my short campaign.

CHAPTER 14

Homeward

Some few of the worst cases were taken on shore, and I sent a card to my brother officers to announce my arrival. B—— and R—— came off to see me immediately; K—— was not at home, but came to me in the evening. He was looking very well, and cheered me by his usual excellent spirits: his wound was nearly well, and he sat by my bedside and had a long chat, as we used to do in camp. It gave us great pleasure to see one another again, and I was glad to find my other brother officers likewise improving. B—— told me there was only one other officer in his room, Dr. C——, our assistant-surgeon, and it was decided that I was to occupy a part of it. They gave but a poor account of Major S—— and B——, whose wounds seemed to have taken an unfavourable turn.

On the 23rd, Major Campbell, the quartermaster-general at Scutari, came off, very kindly, to see me, and recommended me to land at the very first opportunity. It was, however, on that day and the following, too rough to think of doing so, and already one of our boats had been stove-in on the beach. Christmas Day being very fine, B—— and R—— kindly came off to me, and I went ashore with them to their quarters. On the way we passed a number of boats belonging to the Allied fleets, and, on inquiry, found that the body of Brigadier-General Adams was being conveyed on board the *Ripon*, to proceed to England. A guard of honour was also on the wharf, together with crowds of people.

A steep ascent led us to the barrack; and after passing into it through the archway, we turned up some steps, at the top of which was a long corridor, with windows on one side and rooms on the other. The floor was of tiles; and groups of soldiers, in hospital-dress, were lounging about on the sacks of rice which were stored in the passage. We soon arrived at our room, which was of a good size, having two windows, and looking out on the sparkling Bosphorus and Constantinople. The floor was covered with matting; and the table was a door of one of the cupboards, which was supported by trunks in the centre of the room. My walk had completely knocked me up, and I lay down on a bed quite exhausted.

It being Christmas Day, my brother officers had ordered plum-puddings for the men of our regiment who were ill in barracks, and I begged that I might be allowed to contribute towards it. The poor fellows enjoyed it exceedingly, and it put them in capital spirits. It was agreed that we should dine together in our room, and, at five o'clock, a most sumptuous repast was spread on the boards, consisting of soup, turkey, curry, plum-pudding, and jelly; it was all cooked in the "Times" kitchen free of charge. We drank a glass to the health of absent friends; and my worthy companions did not forget to make a bowl of punch for our servants.

They went over in the evening to see poor S———, who was in the hospital, at some little distance from the barrack; and they seemed to think, on their return, that there was but little hope of his recovery. This threw a gloom over the rest of the evening, and we grieved to think we must part with one for whom we had so much regard. My camp-bed was put together, and I lay down thoroughly tired out, and suffering much from cough and rheumatism. I felt however most happy and thankful at having a roof over my head, and at being surrounded by my kind and attentive brother officers, to whom I shall ever feel grateful for their very great kindness. K——— was engaged to dine on board one of H.M. ships at Constantinople, and could not join our Christmas party.

On the 26th B—— went to the hospital to see poor Sharpe, and found him sinking rapidly, his wound having assumed a still more unfavourable aspect. He died on the 28th December. We all deeply lamented his sad death, which was a loss not only to ourselves personally, but also to the service.

K—— came off to see me, and Dr. R—— and other medical men were very attentive and kind; but it was considered by them that my constitution had been much impaired, and that it would be some time before I gained my usual strength, or should be fit to resume active service. Consequently I was ordered before a Medical Board on the 29th, when it was determined that I was to proceed to England for the recovery of my health. On the 30th Major Sharpe was buried in the military burying-ground at Scutari, and his remains were followed to the grave by all his brother officers who were well enough to attend. Forty men were buried this day in one grave, and sixty the day before.

My dinner during my stay at Scutari was always supplied from the "Times" kitchen. I could get soups, jellies, and blanc-mange, as well as anything I required to be cooked. How happy were we to be able to procure such luxuries f I cannot be too thankful or speak too highly of this generous institution. Nothing could have been better organized and arranged; and all who derived benefit from it will feel grateful to those who contributed so generously towards the fund, as well as to the newspaper which evoked the sympathies of the public.

My illness prevented my going into the wards and rooms and visiting the sick, and I was obliged to remain patiently in my very comfortable quarters. I heard great praises of Miss Nightingale.

Her kindness and the attention of the nurses cheered the poor sufferers in the hospital, the condition of which greatly improved after their arrival. We had many books which were supplied by the chaplain, who had charge of the library, and which had been sent from England by our kind and thoughtful countrymen. From our room we could see the Sea of Marmora and the Seraglio Gardens: steamers and transports lay at anchor just below us, embarking or disembarking invalid soldiers from the Crimea. I never witnessed a more beautiful sight than we had from our room when the sun was rising on this splendid city.

I received a letter to say that 220 flannel shirts had been sent out by my kind friend Lady D—— and other ladies of Devonshire, for the use of the men of the 20th Regiment.

On the 31st December an order was sent to me for a passage in the steamer *Tamar* to England, and on the morning of the 1st January, 1855, I walked down to the wharf with Captain B——, and taking a *caique* proceeded to the ship, which was lying in the Golden Horn. Kekewich was busy in the bazaars buying curiosities for me to take to England, and I heard of him galloping about the streets at a tremendous pace, to the consternation of many an old Turk. He brought all that I required in the afternoon, having taken great trouble and shown excellent taste in his selection of articles. I bade him a hearty goodbye, and exceedingly regretted to part with him.

We sailed on the 2nd, and anchored off Scutari to wait for His Royal Highness the Duke of Cambridge, who was going to Malta with his staff in our ship; and at four o'clock the Ambassador's *caique* hove in sight, with the Duke on board. Several officers were also going to England, and we sailed at twelve p.m., in order to make the Dardanelles at daylight.

Our ship was rather a cold one, and the only stove was in the ladies' cabin; but we frequently visited the galley-fire, where was a very amusing cook, who fed us uncommonly well. We had a beautiful sail through the Dardanelles, but outside found a heavy sea running, of which our good ship made the most, as she was a tremendous roller and very fast.

At nine a.m. on the 6th we arrived at Malta, when Admiral Stewart came on board to pay his respects to his Royal Highness, and informed the captain of the *Tamar* that she was to go to Marseilles and take up French troops for the Crimea. He gave the invalid officers leave to go in the ship to Marseilles, but the men, a hundred of whom were on board, he sent to another vessel. It was remarkable how quickly the Maltese coal a ship, for we were at sea at ten p.m., having only been twelve hours at Malta. I found the climate of Malta so truly different from what it was in summer, and the town so much cleaner, that it quite charmed me. I felt much better directly I arrived there, though I soon got very tired of walking about, and returned to the ship.

On my way I passed huge baskets of oranges with leaves on their stems to show their freshness, and I filled my pockets for sixpence, and found them delicious. The trees in the ditch round the town were covered with fruit, and the perfume was most fragrant. It was a lovely, tranquil night when we left Malta, and scarcely a ripple was on the water. The moon was shining brightly, and our fast ship glided along at fourteen miles an hour.

We arrived at Marseilles in sixty hours, after a delightful passage, having passed the Straits of Bonifacio and the island of Sardinia, which are particularly wild and beautiful. On entering the harbour we found it crowded with English steamers waiting to take French soldiers to the seat of war, with stores for their troops.

We did not obtain our *pratique* until two o'clock on the 9th, when, with much trouble, we passed the little baggage we had through the Customs, and at seven p.m. started for England, which I reached on the 12th of January. I travelled with several officers, who proved most agreeable companions. We were for a part of the way accompanied by a Mr. B——, who had a cocked-hat case with him,—an empty one, I believe,—which he said he carried to give himself importance.

CHAPTER 15

Conclusions

Before I conclude, I beg to say that I have purposely avoided, as much as possible, saying anything respecting the management of the war. Before long the result of the present investigation will be published in the shape of a "Blue-book;" and although the inquiry cannot, in fairness, be deemed altogether satisfactory until many of those now in the Crimea have been examined, and especially that gallant general to whom, the whole expedition has been entrusted, the public will form their own judgement from the report of the committee now sitting. It would ill become me, therefore, to dilate upon the subject of their inquiry.

Criticism and abuse have been unsparingly lavished on our rulers, both military and civil, and I hope that it may ultimately be discovered who have been justly, who unjustly, blamed; and who, perhaps deserving the greatest censure, have hitherto altogether escaped it. Certain it is that England ought to blame herself for much that has happened. She remained far too long blind to the aggrandising and encroaching policy of the Czar; she forgot that "*Vestigia nulla retrorsum*" was his motto. The subjection of Finland and Poland had taught her no lesson; and it was not until the eve of the declaration of war, that she was roused from her sleep, and began to believe it possible that a forty years' peace could be disturbed. It was not until after the massacre of Sinope, that the people or Government of England would believe that the Emperor's reply to the summons of the

Western Powers could be unfavourable; but soon after this summons was sent, the publication of those memorable secret despatches unmasked the aggrandising spirit of Nicholas, and the people of England almost unanimously declared themselves in favour of war.

Whether the Czar would or would not have returned a different reply to our summons, if our Ministers had adopted a more threatening tone, it is now impossible to ascertain; but there can be no doubt that they, at all events, did their utmost to avert the impending war, though many may think that they used the wrong means. However they may have been blamed, facts appear to prove that system and routine have been more at fault than men; and probably the same mistakes would have been made, and the same sufferings would have been endured, if those who raised the greatest clamour against the Ministers had themselves been at the helm.

For many previous years, while reforms of almost every other kind had been demanded and obtained by the people, and while every other science had been cultivated, England had forgotten the now often quoted axiom, "*Si vis pacem, bellum para*:" she had almost entirely neglected the arts of war. Suddenly our people saw that the Czar really had designs upon Constantinople; and though they were possibly more anxious, on their own account, to prevent Russian encroachment, than to protect a falling state, they were one and all determined to repel the Northern invader. Our armies and fleets were suddenly expected "to come, to see, to conquer." They were told to invade the territory of one who had been long making every preparation, and collecting every warlike appliance for the deadly struggle; and they were expected to take, in a few hours or days, the stronghold which Russia had for years been endeavouring to render impregnable.

Our fleet and army have indeed done their duty nobly. It was no fault of our brave soldiers that they were landed at Gallipoli, or that they were laid low by pestilence at Devna or Varna: they only obeyed orders. At last they sailed eagerly for the Crimea; they fought and won great battles against fearful odds; opposed a foe who was fighting for his native soil; and they have perhaps done more in the same space of time than any other army did before. Their loss has however been severe. Winds and waves have spent their fury upon them; their ships, their clothes, their comforts, have been lost; pestilence has thinned their ranks; and there now remains, alas! But a small portion of that magnificent army which so short a time ago left these shores full of life, hope, and energy.

England bewails this loss, but is her grief equal to her disappointment? Were not the miseries of Devna obliterated for a time by the triumphs of Alma? She is indeed mortified and disappointed, because our army and that of our gallant allies are still before Sebastopol, and because that stronghold still remains uncaptured. Let us hope that experience has taught us, however dearly, many of the numerous errors of our system, and that these will be promptly remedied. Certain it is, that with the aid of the God of battles (without whose aid we can indeed do nothing) our brave soldiers and sailors will, whenever it is required of them, do whatever man can do; and our arms will, with the Divine blessing, ultimately obtain that triumph to which the justice of our cause so folly entitles them.

The great Disturber of Peace being now no more, let us hope that his death may be more valuable than his life, and that his successor may listen, before it be too late, to the proposals of the Plenipotentiaries of the Allied Powers, now assembled at Vienna; and that such a peace may be established as may long secure Europe against further encroachment and bloodshed. It may however be vain to expect this from one, the first act of whose reign was to proclaim to his subjects, that he intends to continue the policy of Peter, of Catherine, of Alexander, and of his father.

One sad word more, and I have done. But a few days ago I heard of the death of my dear friend and brother officer Kekewich, whom I have so often mentioned in these pages, and I cannot conclude my task without offering my humble tribute to his memory. I loved him not only because he was the brother of my dear sister's husband, but for his own sake: he was my messmate and companion from the time we embarked at Plymouth until he was wounded at Inkermann. We drank out of the same cup; the same blanket covered us; on the same pillow our heads rested. Through the many perils and hardships of camp life, I had good opportunities of judging of his worth, and I may say, without exaggeration, that a kinder friend, or a braver young soldier, never existed. His voice always cheered me, and indeed all who heard it; and his attention to me when I was ill was greater than I can express. He joined our regiment long before he was obliged to do so, a few weeks previous to our sailing, and it was not long before he was beloved by every officer or soldier who knew him.

He received his lieutenancy, without purchase, soon after he had gone to Scutari to recover from his wound. Here his kind and generous disposition did not fail to show itself; and a letter which his brother tells me has been received from Mrs. H—— expresses her extreme gratitude for his having nursed her son in his last hours. There is much reason to suppose that he caught the fever from which he died, while engaged at the hospital in one of these acts of kindness. He had recovered from his wound, and he went to Corfu, in charge of convalescents, when he ought to have remained in bed. On his arrival he was most kindly received into the house of Colonel Walpole, D.Q.G., where every attention, every comfort was bestowed upon him. There was, however, at the time of his landing, little expectation of his recovery, and he breathed his last on the 16th of February, 1855.

Thus died one of the most promising young officers in the British army. No one seemed, from his strength of form and constitution, more likely to get over the fever and dysentery which attacked him; but it was not the will of God that it should be so. His remains were carried on a gun-carriage to the military cemetery at Corfu, on the 19th of February, followed by every military and naval officer in the garrison.

And now, Reader, farewell!

ALSO FROM LEONAUR
AVAILABLE IN SOFTCOVER OR HARDCOVER WITH DUST JACKET

CAPTAIN OF THE 95th (Rifles) *by Jonathan Leach*—An officer of Wellington's Sharpshooters during the Peninsular, South of France and Waterloo Campaigns of the Napoleonic Wars.

BUGLER AND OFFICER OF THE RIFLES *by William Green & Harry Smith* With the 95th (Rifles) during the Peninsular & Waterloo Campaigns of the Napoleonic Wars

BAYONETS, BUGLES AND BONNETS *by James 'Thomas' Todd*—Experiences of hard soldiering with the 71st Foot - the Highland Light Infantry - through many battles of the Napoleonic wars including the Peninsular & Waterloo Campaigns

THE ADVENTURES OF A LIGHT DRAGOON *by George Farmer & G.R. Gleig*—A cavalryman during the Peninsular & Waterloo Campaigns, in captivity & at the siege of Bhurtpore, India

THE COMPLEAT RIFLEMAN HARRIS *by Benjamin Harris as told to & transcribed by Captain Henry Curling*—The adventures of a soldier of the 95th (Rifles) during the Peninsular Campaign of the Napoleonic Wars

WITH WELLINGTON'S LIGHT CAVALRY *by William Tomkinson*—The Experiences of an officer of the 16th Light Dragoons in the Peninsular and Waterloo campaigns of the Napoleonic Wars.

SURTEES OF THE RIFLES *by William Surtees*—A Soldier of the 95th (Rifles) in the Peninsular campaign of the Napoleonic Wars.

ENSIGN BELL IN THE PENINSULAR WAR *by George Bell*—The Experiences of a young British Soldier of the 34th Regiment 'The Cumberland Gentlemen' in the Napoleonic wars.

WITH THE LIGHT DIVISION *by John H. Cooke*—The Experiences of an Officer of the 43rd Light Infantry in the Peninsula and South of France During the Napoleonic Wars

NAPOLEON'S IMPERIAL GUARD: FROM MARENGO TO WATERLOO *by J. T. Headley*—This is the story of Napoleon's Imperial Guard from the bearskin caps of the grenadiers to the flamboyance of their mounted chasseurs, their principal characters and the men who commanded them.

BATTLES & SIEGES OF THE PENINSULAR WAR *by W. H. Fitchett*—Corunna, Busaco, Albuera, Ciudad Rodrigo, Badajos, Salamanca, San Sebastian & Others

AVAILABLE ONLINE AT **www.leonaur.com**
AND OTHER GOOD BOOK STORES

ALSO FROM LEONAUR
AVAILABLE IN SOFTCOVER OR HARDCOVER WITH DUST JACKET

WELLINGTON AND THE PYRENEES CAMPAIGN VOLUME I: FROM VITORIA TO THE BIDASSOA by *F. C. Beatson*—The final phase of the campaign in the Iberian Peninsula.

WELLINGTON AND THE INVASION OF FRANCE VOLUME II: THE BIDASSOA TO THE BATTLE OF THE NIVELLE by *F. C. Beatson*—The second of Beatson's series on the fall of Revolutionary France published by Leonaur, the reader is once again taken into the centre of Wellington's strategic and tactical genius.

WELLINGTON AND THE FALL OF FRANCE VOLUME III: THE GAVES AND THE BATTLE OF ORTHEZ by *F. C. Beatson*—This final chapter of F. C. Beatson's brilliant trilogy shows the 'captain of the age' at his most inspired and makes all three books essential additions to any Peninsular War library.

NAVAL BATTLES OF THE NAPOLEONIC WARS by *W. H. Fitchett*—Cape St. Vincent, the Nile, Cadiz, Copenhagen, Trafalgar & Others

SERGEANT GUILLEMARD: THE MAN WHO SHOT NELSON? by *Robert Guillemard*—A Soldier of the Infantry of the French Army of Napoleon on Campaign Throughout Europe

WITH THE GUARDS ACROSS THE PYRENEES by *Robert Batty*—The Experiences of a British Officer of Wellington's Army During the Battles for the Fall of Napoleonic France, 1813.

A STAFF OFFICER IN THE PENINSULA by *E. W. Buckham*—An Officer of the British Staff Corps Cavalry During the Peninsula Campaign of the Napoleonic Wars

THE LEIPZIG CAMPAIGN: 1813—NAPOLEON AND THE "BATTLE OF THE NATIONS" by *F. N. Maude*—Colonel Maude's analysis of Napoleon's campaign of 1813.

BUGEAUD: A PACK WITH A BATON by *Thomas Robert Bugeaud*—The Early Campaigns of a Soldier of Napoleon's Army Who Would Become a Marshal of France.

TWO LEONAUR ORIGINALS

SERGEANT NICOL by *Daniel Nicol*—The Experiences of a Gordon Highlander During the Napoleonic Wars in Egypt, the Peninsula and France.

WATERLOO RECOLLECTIONS by *Frederick Llewellyn*—Rare First Hand Accounts, Letters, Reports and Retellings from the Campaign of 1815.

AVAILABLE ONLINE AT **www.leonaur.com**
AND OTHER GOOD BOOK STORES

www.ingramcontent.com/pod-product-compliance
Lightning Source LLC
Chambersburg PA
CBHW021004090426
42738CB00007B/653